ADVENTURE TRAVEL IN THE
THIRD WORLD

The authors make no guarantee that readers of this book will be able to travel safely and problem-free using the methods described herein. Although the information in this book is accurate and has been tested by the authors (unless otherwise noted), every travel and/or survival situation is not the same. Information and techniques presented herein reflect the authors' individual beliefs and experiences which the reader cannot duplicate exactly, and said information and techniques can be potentially dangerous and could result in serious injury, death, or criminal liability. Therefore, the authors, publisher, and distributors of this book disclaim any liability from any damage or injuries of any type that a reader or user of information contained in this book may incur. Travel at your own risk!

ADVENTURE TRAVEL IN THE
THIRD WORLD

Everything You Need to Know to Survive in Remote and Hostile Destinations

Foreword by Robert Young Pelton
author of the best selling *The World's Most Dangerous Places*

NIAGARA COLLEGE LRC

Jeff Randall and Mike Perrin

Paladin Press • Boulder, Colorado

We are the men of intrinsic value, who can strike our fortunes out of ourselves, whose worth is independent of accidents in life, or revolutions in government: we have heads to get money, and hearts to spend it.

George Farquhar

extreme \ik-'strēm\ *(adjective)*—going far beyond what is reasonable or normal

adventurer \əd-'ven-ch(ə-)rer\ *(noun)*—somebody who takes part in exciting or risky activities

DEDICATION

To Carl—thanks for the wisdom. And to our family, friends, and team members of Randall's Adventure & Training.

Just before this book was sent to the publisher, we learned that a close friend of ours, Adolfo Preuss, died in a small plane crash in the jungles of Costa Rica. The Sansa flight into Puerto Jimenez was carrying six passengers and two crewmen. Adolfo, the pilot, and the copilot all died in the crash; the remaining passengers survived and were rescued.

This is a heartbreaking loss for the authors. We have taken this same flight on numerous occasions to visit and work with Adolfo. He was not only the best indigenous guide we have ever worked with, he was also considered family. We have decided to leave Adolfo's citation in the Acknowledgments and Resources chapter as it was originally written not only to honor him in his untimely death but also in hopes that those reading this book will decide to travel to the Ona Peninsula area of Costa Rica and experience a part of the world that Adolfo made famous.

Rest in peace, Adolfo. Your wisdom, wit, and integrity will be missed. Hopefully someday we will once again be able to sit around a jungle lodge drinking beer and listening to Stevie Ray Vaughn on the portable CD player.

Sus amigos,
Randall's Adventure & Training

Adventure Travel in the Third World:
Everything You Need to Know to Survive in Remote and Hostile Destinations
by Jeff Randall and Mike Perrin

ISBN 1-58160-381-9
Printed in the United States of America

Published by Paladin Press, a division of
Paladin Enterprises, Inc.
Gunbarrel Tech Center
7077 Winchester Circle
Boulder, Colorado 80301 USA
+1.303.443.7250

Direct inquiries and/or orders to the above address.

Visit our Web site at www.paladin-press.com

On the cover: Dr. Robert Schertz paddles his raft down an Amazon tributary during an adventure with the authors. Cover photo by Jeff Randall.

Unless otherwise noted, all photos are © Jeff Randall and Mike Perrin.

Contents

Foreword

Survival is a misunderstood term. To some it means "not dying." To others it means figuring out how to cook other members of a rugby team on a windswept Andean mountainside. To a few it means what it should: To live better. To rise above. To do more than just live.

The idea of survival is not just to live but to live well.

Ever notice how some people will buy all sorts of gear and provisions and then pay big bucks to learn how to survive in places where the locals wear just a loincloth and a smile? Ever watch those TV shows that pay a million dollars if you can hold out for a month in certain locales, places where some people shell out lots of money to vacation? If you know what I mean, you will understand how one man's hell can be another man's paradise. The difference is knowledge.

Sure, you can go out and buy any number of survival guides written by people who actually tell you to read warnings on coffee cups. You could also spend a few years in the jungle on your own learning bush lore from the local tribes. But there is a happy medium: this book. It is the distillation of years of real experience crammed into an easy-to-read guide, the condensed equivalent of a few thousand miles of hard travel, bruises, and screw-ups laid out for your enjoyment, entertainment, and edification.

It is sad that we have lost a lot of the normal street smarts and bush skills that humans had always learned through the course of their lives. These days, most of us can survive the daily grind armed with only a cell phone and a credit card. Our biggest survival problem might be the cable TV not working or our inability to find a good mechanic. We have pretty much taken care of any inconvenience or danger that might ruffle our well-run day. Then, BLAM, things suddenly go sideways. It doesn't matter if you are in Manhattan or the Amazon River basin.

Even if you aren't worried about catastrophe, you should worry about handling minor and major misadventures. And if you think you are immune from misfortune, then you should enjoy learning the basic skills that let you enjoy remote regions and the wilderness. The best way not only to learn but to enjoy survival is to travel to places where a survival manual is a curiosity and a first-aid kit is a luxury. Here you can put yourself to the test and learn that having basic bush skills, street smarts, and self-confidence can go a long way in making sure you stay healthy and happy. Before you learn the hard way, though, make sure you get advice from people who have been there, done that.

How will you know these folks? Easy. You'll bump into these experts in the most remote and dangerous parts of the world and, despite the inclement conditions, they will be— *gasp*—smiling. They have the nerve to be relaxed, comfortable, and . . . enjoying themselves. Are they nuts? Don't they know that it's *dangerous*? Well, sure, they do . . . but it's not dangerous for them.

You see, the secret to staying healthy, happy, and at home in remote and dangerous places is having enough knowledge to relax. If you are aware of the dangers and know how to handle them, you can concentrate on the pleasures and attractions. You get that level of confidence by attending the school of hard knocks . . . or by hanging out with celebrated graduates.

Jeff Randall and Mike Perrin are two guys you want to hang out with because they make the survival game fun. To them, survival is not showing how tough you are but how smart and relaxed you are.

So take it from me. Read this book. Then see if you can get in on one of their trips or classes and make the valley of death your next vacation spot.

—Robert Young Pelton

Author, *The World's Most Dangerous Places* and *Come Back Alive*

Introduction: Living to Tell the Stories

I have lived my life searching for truth—not the biased "truth" reported by major news outlets or simple facts confined to the pages of a nonfiction book. My life's mission has been to see and experience things for myself; to learn what's truly contained in the world outside the borders of my home country. Throughout my travels into foreign and sometimes hostile lands, one thing has always stood clear in a sea of uncertainty: Except for subtle differences in culture and situations, people are pretty much the same the world over. How we react to these differences is usually the determining factor when it comes to surviving.

During my travels I have seen countries in revolution, traveled with drug smugglers who made a living processing cocaine in discreet jungle labs, shared beers with Third World rebels, worked side by side with foreign militaries, led major media film crews into dangerous places, had shotguns pressed against my head by folks who didn't want me in their world, been on a plane that had a bomb attempt against it, survived for weeks in jungles with little food or fresh water, fought with and subdued an irate passenger for a major airline during a flight over the Pacific Ocean, had a front row seat to watch Peruvian Special Forces take down the Marxist group Tupac Amaru in the Japanese Embassy, been the recipient of numerous threats and prices placed on my head by jealous Americans operating in foreign countries, and been told to "never come back" more times than I can count. All of this I have done as a civilian traveler in search of adventure and knowledge.

Why is it that some travelers can be introduced to Hell and live to tell the stories, while others seem to find bad luck during a simple pleasure vacation? It is certainly true that some people, through no fault of their own, just get caught in the wrong place at the wrong time. The consequences of these mishaps can range from legal problems and injury to kidnapping and, in the most extreme incidents, death. Without a doubt some situations are unavoidable, but the majority simply turned bad because of the travelers' lack of research, poor awareness of their circumstances and surroundings, or indecisiveness when faced with crisis.

Perhaps the greatest reason for bad travel experiences is the seemingly inherent egotistical attitude of being from the United States or some other "developed" country. Our unique reluctance to swallow our pride and our distinct ability to judge the rest of the world based on our set of values and laws have, without a doubt, caused more problems for Americans overseas than any other.

Having traveled for many years in remote regions, my co-author and partner, Mike Perrin, and I decided it was time for a straightforward book on adventure travel and managing the risks associated with it. Through our travels, we learned that there are many exciting places and good people and an abundance of untapped knowledge in the world, regardless of the location or its reputation. To restrict our experiences because of risks and uncertainties would be as great a crime as not offering what we have learned to other adventurers and free spirits of the world.

We travel as seekers of knowledge, nothing more. We do not place right-or-wrong judgment on the coca farmer who makes a living for his family by the only means he knows, nor do we judge the system intent on shutting down his operation. Simply put, it is not our business. Worldwide adventure travel is an education and must remain neutral and fun. To use it for anything other than that is an expedient way to shorten the number of breaths you will take in your life.

As of this writing, neither Mike nor I have ever graduated from a college, written a book, been in the military, worked for any government agency, killed anyone, spent time in prison, or have any other unique qualification that many readers expect from those who author adventure travel "guide" books. After this shocking revelation, some of you may decide to quit reading right now. So be it. Throughout our adventures, we have learned that those who travel to feed their ego or who portray themselves as something other than what they are usually end up being poor adventure travelers. At best they will only make their traveling companions miserable, and at worst they will offend the indigenous people of the host country, thereby endangering not only their own lives but their companions' as well.

This book focuses on travel in the Third World, countries in transition, and tropical wilderness and jungles. It is designed to be a quick-read survival guide for the first-time overseas adventurer. It will take you from the planning and risk assessment stage on the front end of a trip, through how to handle situations that can arise during the trip, and all the way back home again. The stories and information provided are factual, although some locations and names have been altered to protect the innocent, the guilty, and our overseas network.

Although this book offers techniques that have been applied time and time again during our journeys, we do not expect it to become the bible of adventure travel. Instead, it is simply meant to be a common-sense foundation on which adventurers can build and expand during their travels.

It is important to note here that no person or book can cover all contingencies that may arise when you take the path less traveled. Unexpected events are an inherent part of any trip. The only thing certain is that the unexpected can and will happen, which is the very definition of adventure travel. In this book, we tell you what combination of factors enabled us to deal with the unexpected. Such situations must be handled with a combination of learned knowledge, intuitive thinking, common sense, and wit. We can help you with everything except the common sense and wit. In the end, all we expect from the reader is to use what he or she can and discard the rest, but if the information offered within these pages gives one person the ability to live through a situation and return home to tell the story, then it has been a success.

—Jeff Randall

CHAPTER 1

Destination Research

"I want to go where tourists don't go."

Those are the challenge words we often say to our-selves when looking for an adventure vacation. The tour groups with little blue-haired ladies and the worn-out des-tinations full of tourist-junk hawkers hold no allure. Yet the places to go for adventure travel have extreme envi-ronments, unrelenting pests, unpredictable weather, polit-ical turmoil, and, for the most part, are devoid of modern amenities. The mosquitos and chiggers defy repellent, the cops carry AK-47s and Uzis, local law is the only law, and the only part of the trip that has the possibility of going as planned is arriving and leaving the host country on time—and even that is not guaranteed.

So, if you are going to go "where tourists don't go," your survival depends a great deal on how well you do your homework up front. Natural disasters, terrorist activity, volatile elections, revolution, and civil war all have some-thing in common: They each can turn a nice, friendly coun-try into a not-so-friendly country overnight. Therefore, your research needs to be up-to-date and accurate.

Don't rely on a travel agent or friend to do this work for you. They aren't going on your trip—you are. What your neighbor told you about Haiti or Sierra Leone when he had such a wonderful time there a few years back may not be true today. Failing to do your own detailed research on your destination—and all stops in between—is not only inexcus-able, it's downright stupid.

Valuable research tools include the Internet, news reports, and other travelers who have been to your destina-tion area *recently*. The Internet in particular has become a tremendous asset for travelers. With it you can check the U.S. State Department Consular Information Sheets and Travel Warnings for just about anywhere in the world at http://travel.state.gov/. (For those of you without Internet access, the mailing address to request these reports is U.S. Department of State, 2201 C Street NW, Washington, D.C., 20520.) The consular report will give you a general view of the political climate in your destination country, although this source has a tendency to be less than current due to the ever-changing political scene in many places.

Pay attention to news reports that pertain to your destination or layover in between. Despite our disrespect for much of today's news media, it is still the most readily available source of current information for a country or region. Keeping an eye on the "unimportant" stories buried deep in the papers is a great way of predicting potential problems when traveling to the Third World. The only better source would be a phone call to a person on the ground where you are going.

You must, of course, check out the obvious, such as laws, customs, and visa requirements, and you will certainly want to look into the fun and adventurous things you will enjoy on your trip. But do not overlook the not-so-fun and not-so-obvious. Political unrest, crime, areas to avoid, strict laws coupled with corrupt officials who view travelers as an opportunity for quick cash, or maybe that "dormant" volcano that's about ready to pop should all be considered in your travel planning. Some countries retain prejudices against certain nationalities, genders, or races. (Yes, there are still people in some countries who don't hide their dislike for blacks, Asians, Europeans, Americans, or whoever.) Doing such research here, on the front end, and getting as close to your destination in knowledge without actually going there is time well-spent.

It's obviously going to be risky if your destination country is experiencing a civil war, but what about those countries that appear docile at the moment? Have you checked to see if there is a contentious election coming up, or perhaps labor protests that could change the political climate quickly? Or maybe your destination country is not on the best of terms with the United States, thus creating a very anti-American sentiment. You need to know these sorts of things so you will be able to recognize and avoid potentially dangerous situations before they erupt.

If you have the contacts, local street gossip is an excel-

In Third World countries, hotly debated elections can change
a normally peaceful society into a volatile eruption overnight.

lent source of useful information. (Never forget that rumor
is almost always premature fact.) Look to trustworthy
friends, acquaintances, and others who frequent the country for business, family, or recreation purposes. Getting such
gossip from an unfamiliar hotel or guide at your destination
may not be the best course of action, though. Remember,
they want your dollars and are usually going to downplay
any problems. If, however, you have an on-the-ground
guide or source that you know and have done business with
in the past, then he will usually be reliable. What's the difference? If he knows you as a repeat customer, he will want
to keep your dollars returning. Steering you into a dangerous situation would be a detriment to his future income.

The bottom line here is this: Don't go into your trip with

rose-colored glasses on and let the bad side of paradise catch you off guard.

LAWS AND POLITICAL STATUS

Amazingly, many travelers have been surprised to find out that their own country's laws do not extend beyond the borders of the United States or wherever they may be from. Some of these people are currently serving out harsh sentences in Third World, puke-box prisons because of ignorance of the laws of the country they were visiting or the presumption that their U.S. or European citizenship gave them immunity from mistakes. Well, there is a well-worn cliche that applies here as well as anywhere abroad: "Ignorance of the law is no excuse."

When you enter another country, you are subject to *its* laws, rules, and regulations. Whether they enforce them to the letter is totally left to their discretion and whim, especially in the Third World, where economies are often desperate. But you don't want to take that chance. To cite one obvious example, drug smuggling is frowned upon abroad as much as it is in the United States, but usually the consequences are much harsher if you are arrested for it while overseas. Just because the locals have easy access to hashish or other drugs doesn't mean you are free to indulge in its transportation or use.

If you commit a serious offense or even look like you have done something wrong while overseas, such lofty concepts as "your rights" and being "presumed innocent until proven guilty" simply do not apply. You may have only been a bystander at the wrong place and time, but you could still be arrested on suspicion of involvement. If you are not careful, this paradise-vacation-turned-nightmare scenario can happen anywhere, anytime.

The positive aspect to your ignorance of the law in Third World countries is that most officials are happy to have your U.S. dollars, so they will frequently overlook minor infractions so long as you are polite and offer to pay for any inconvenience you may have caused.

LANGUAGE

Several years ago I went to a Latin American country on a bush expedition. I knew very little Spanish at the time. I ran out of cigarettes while we were traveling for days on rivers, and I convinced the boat driver to pull over at a small village so I could try to obtain a pack of smokes.

I left the boat by myself and went over the hill into the village, putting myself out of sight of the boat and my friends. After spending about five minutes trying to get the villagers to understand what I wanted to buy, I realized they thought I wanted to *give* them cigarettes, not buy some. I also realized at this point that every man in the village was now gathering around me in anticipation of their free cigarette, and many were well intoxicated.

I finally threw up my hands, smiled, and turned back toward the boat. They followed closely, and one began shouting at me in Spanish when he realized I wasn't going to hand out cigarettes. When my friends saw me come over the hill to re-embark, I was at a full run with half the village on my tail and the drunk still shouting at me. I made the boat and we quickly departed as the drunk began throwing rocks at us. This misunderstanding could have easily been averted if I had simply known a few common Spanish phrases.

Not knowing the language of the host country is not the end of the world, nor will it necessarily ruin your trip, but it will make your life much easier and your time more enjoyable if you can learn at least some key words and phrases. It will also avert a lot of problems from scam artists who look for tourists who don't know the language. How so? You may think your newfound friend is discussing the best route to your hotel with the cab driver, but he actually may be setting you up for a robbery with the driver's assistance. Another example: Guides sometimes negotiate arrangements and prices "on the fly" with other service providers. By understanding some of the language, you may find out that your guide will actually accept less money than he's asking of you, or you may catch him padding the cost of something in order to give himself an under-the-table cut of the deal.

If you can learn 100 basic words in any language, you can survive in countries where it is spoken. Once you have memorized these words, then learn to string them together into simple phrases like, "Where is the bathroom/airport/hotel/police?", "How much does it cost?", "Please slow down," "Can I buy you a beer?", and, of course, "Would you like a cigarette?"

Don't worry about being fluent with your sentences; your key words and phrases along with gestures and other body language will get your point across fairly well. If you plan on carrying an electronic phrase book or dictionary, back it up with a print copy because dead batteries, moisture, and breakage may leave you speechless. Have no fear, though—no matter where your travels take you, there always seems to be someone who speaks English or at least understands enough to help.

With language, the golden rule for travelers is to never, ever pretend you understand something if you do not. You will see this advice over and over in this book, because to do so can land you in a world of trouble. If you don't understand and try to be cool and "worldly" by nodding comprehension, you may find that you have hired your guide's entire family, or he may show up that night at your room with the "ladies" you agreed to. If you don't understand, just say so. Don't shout or raise your voice. That is a sure way to offend most folks just like in the United States or your own country.

Keep conversation light, especially if you are lean on knowing the language and customs. We have a hard-and-fast rule that we insist on when traveling to other countries:

Never make conversation about religion or politics. At the least you will offend someone, and in Third World countries these two topics can easily get you killed. Don't even joke about the Taliban or Sendero Luminoso (better known as Shining Path) among yourselves in a café. The old saying "the walls have ears" is very true. An eavesdropper at the next table may only hear one or two key words, and the next thing you know you're explaining to the police who you are and why you are there.

Be careful not to use slang terms you use in day-to-day conversation at home. With few exceptions, slang doesn't translate well and can easily result in insulting the local you are speaking with. Even those who know English sometimes don't get the slang and won't understand when you say something like "Hey, don't get your panties in a wad," or "It ain't worth getting bent out of shape over." They will usually just smile politely and start talking about something else, never telling you they had no clue what you meant.

The same is true of jokes. Most jokes don't translate worth a damn . . . unless the joke is on you; then the locals will see the humor every time.

Communication confusion can extend beyond spoken language. The first time I visited the backwoods of South America, I brought all of my hometown charm with me and received many laughs, giggles, and confused looks in response. On one occasion we were sitting at an open-air café along the Amazon River, and our guide's nephews kept laughing at me and whispering to each other every time I said "OK" and made the familiar circled finger gesture when I said it. They then pointed to the young boy cooking in the kitchen and said "OK," repeating the gesture I had made. I then noticed the cook smiling rather amorously at me and our guide laughing so hard he was nearly falling out of his chair. It turns out that the little circle we form with our finger in the states signifying "OK" infers something about homosexuality in South America. Moral: Keep your hands in your pockets.

LOCAL CUSTOMS

Although local customs are as varied as the different peoples of the world and usually vary a great deal from region to region within a country, a smile and polite attitude will fit in anywhere. Yet when it comes to customs in other countries, there is one fundamental problem we have noticed over and over again with travelers—they often judge other countries' cultures by their homeland standards. Well, guess what? You're in *their* country, so you must play by their rules, not yours.

For example, we have taken many clients to remote villages in the jungle where custom requires the locals to offer a bowl of homemade brew called *masato*, a fermented, low-alcohol drink made from a plant tuber and the villagers' saliva. Each visitor must drink the entire bowl offered before refusing any more. Not doing so is taken as an insult. The clients who refused the drink were subsequently ignored by the villagers.

If this episode had been a true survival situation, our clients would have *had* to take what the villagers first offered before asking for other aid. If they didn't, they would have left with no assistance from them. Knowing such things beforehand can literally mean the difference between life and death if a situation turns bad.

Putting all of this into perspective, misunderstandings and social faux pas are really not that big a deal in the areas well-traveled by tourists. Those folks are used to rude and stupid travelers and smile anyway. But the more you travel to places "where tourists don't go," you will find they take their customs more seriously and are more easily insulted by ignorant or rude behavior. Before you go into less-traveled areas, it would be wise to employ a local guide who can clue you in on what to expect.

Sure, there will be some customs that may irritate you. Women are still considered second-class citizens in much of the underdeveloped world. The championed rights of chil-

The cultures of primitive or indigenous people may appear strange to the adventure traveler. Always research your destination and keep a friendly, nonthreatening attitude when interacting with any new culture.

dren, immigrants, and animals have not found a foothold yet in many Third World countries either. In fact, women and children work hard every day, the house pet is being raised for food, and PETA means "People Eating Tasty Animals." Leave your crusades at home and try to learn about rather than change the local culture and customs.

Here's another example. It is still common in most Central and South American cultures to see close physical contact among family members and friends that American culture has tabooed as a sign of questionable sexual preference. Uncles and nephews will fall asleep together with arms wrapped around each other, and girls who are friends hold hands walking down the street. (I can remember when girlfriends held hands in the United States before they worried someone might think they were lesbians.) If you know about such customs before visiting another country, you will be less likely to do something inappropriate like stare or make a snide comment.

There is one custom that seems to be universal and has been an icebreaker for us in more than one tense situation. Offering up a cigarette or a taste of liquor is still a sign of goodwill in many remote places. (The exception would be an Islamic country, where it could be taken as a serious insult.) Many times when we have encountered a stern, untrusting face who had the power to deny us passage, I would smile real big and hold up a pack of smokes, and instantly the frown turned to a smile and everyone began chattering happily as we all puffed away.

Offering any gift, no matter how small, is generally interpreted as goodwill, but be careful because it can also put the burden of having to give a gift in kind upon the local you are visiting. It can be very humiliating to a villager if he or she doesn't have anything to offer in return. They will not feel quite as obligated by taking a cigarette, but they may offer you their local brew if you give them liquor. Then you must accept or they will be insulted. Accept the consequences of your actions and drink up. The best policy is to think your action through before acting, and have a local with you who can help keep you out of trouble.

So by all means research the local customs before you go, but don't be too concerned about knowing all the idiosyncrasies of the culture. Learning as you go is one of the joys of adventure travel. You are going to make mistakes and embarrass yourself, so relax and get used to it. As long as you are polite and can laugh at yourself, most local people will treat you very well and even go out of their way to help the naive, ignorant, but polite and good-natured tourist.

MEDICAL REQUIREMENTS

Third World medicine is a mixture of good medicine from around 50 years ago and witch doctors, so you are better off taking preventive measures before you depart. Check with your local health department and the U.S. Consular Info Sheet to get required immunizations for your target country. This will usually include yellow fever, tetanus, and typhoid. Hepatitis A and B immunizations are usually required, and you should have them, but know that there are new strains popping up faster than the medical community can develop immunizations. Make sure your tetanus booster is up-to-date, too. If you are using a tour service to help with arrangements, they should be able to provide you with medical requirements for a specific area, but again, it's your responsibility to see to your own welfare.

The standard for malaria prevention has been a "horse" pill called lariam, taken once weekly. There is also the antibiotic doxycycline, taken once a day, that works on some strains, but bear in mind that nothing is guaranteed to prevent malaria every time if the right female mosquito bites you. These drugs can have side effects too. Lariam can cause a rise in blood pressure in some people, and doxycycline makes your skin so sensitive to sunlight that at high altitudes you could become medium rare in about 30 minutes without sunblock on. There is also evidence that both of these drugs can be destructive to your liver with prolonged use. It's not a problem if this is a once-in-a-lifetime trip, but for frequent travelers to tropical regions it is something to consider. That was the primary reason why we stopped taking medication to prevent malaria long ago. Finally, always check with your doctor before taking any medication, especially if you already have heart or blood pressure problems.

Once in-country, you can usually find out pretty quick from local sources if and where there is an outbreak of malaria, dengue, cholera, or other disease and simply avoid those areas. As for the Pandora's box of bacteria and viruses you've never heard of that will assault your system from touchdown to takeoff, we'll cover those later in the book.

All of these medical preparations are for your benefit only. The little health card they give you at the health department with your immunity record on it is basically good for scratch paper. The airlines and your destination country don't care about any of this. Typically, they won't check to see what immunizations you've had or what other health problems you may have. They simply want your money. The only value your immunity record may hold is being able to show a Third World doctor what you have been immunized against.

INSURANCE

Insurance companies are famous for trying to weasel out of paying a claim for an overseas accident, so be sure to check that you are properly covered with all your insurance providers before traveling. You gave them the perfect excuse to reject your claim when you rented that motorcycle in a Third World city, crashed head-on with a local taxi, and did the spastic Olympic gymnast act over the vehicle, breaking four or five bones in the process. Or maybe it was some rare bacteria/spider/snake that bit you and won you a stay in a hospital that resembled a Civil War battlefield surgical unit.

Then there's the whole cornucopia of kidnapping, mugging, and personal injury as a result of criminal and terrorist activity. Your regular health insurance might balk a little while coughing up money for these kinds of things if you don't have explicit coverage for them in your policies.

Most insurance companies realize folks are going to vacation once a year and will cover out-of-the-ordinary claims—but not *too* out of the ordinary. It is very likely you may need an accident rider to get additional coverage for things like climbing mountains, wrestling anacondas, or hiking into an area the U.S. State Department warns to stay out of. It's also wise to check any exclusions you may have on your life insurance policies.

In a few countries, the host government doesn't care if you are insured by Lloyd's of London; they will still require you to purchase their approved state health insurance upon entering their country. It's not terribly expensive, and you really don't have a choice because they won't let you in unless you have it, so just buy it. Some of the former Soviet countries maintain this practice.

Flight insurance that covers you and your baggage is an option, but in all the trips we've made we've never lost luggage. Being aware and practicing common-sense security has kept our bags intact and with us. All insurance papers should be at home with someone you trust, but be sure to keep the contact information and policy numbers with you on the road in case you need to report an accident or make a claim immediately.

PASSPORT AND VISA REQUIREMENTS

There are about 4,500 places nationwide where you can apply for a passport, and it will take three to six weeks to obtain one. Check the U.S. government listings in your phone book or the U.S. State Department's Web site for the location nearest you. You'll need a certified birth certificate, a photo ID (driver's license will work), and $65 at the time of this writing.

Some countries also require an entry visa in addition to a passport. The most direct route is to take your passport to the country's embassy in the United States to get the visa, but going in person could mean waiting in a line. Otherwise, you can mail your passport to the embassy for the visa to be stamped inside. There are many companies that specialize in acquiring visas and can greatly expedite this process, though they charge an additional fee for their services.

A travel agent, the consular report, your destination country's U.S. embassy, or an Internet search will tell you which countries require visas for your stay. Get your visa before you leave home because it's doubtful the airline will even let you board without all the right paperwork.

The time it takes to get a visa can vary depending on where you want to go. The politics of your destination country can have a great deal to do with how long it takes or whether you'll get one at all. If you go with a commercial service, they will be able to tell you up front if there is a problem getting a visa for a particular country. All of this should tell you to start working through the passport/visa requirements far in advance of your trip.

Once you get a visa, it is specific for that country. If you have a visa for Belarus, it does not authorize you to go sightseeing across the border in Russia or Ukraine. There are shysters at the borders who claim they can get you a visa for a certain amount of cash, but you'll still be locked up or kicked back across the border if you try to pass on it. This is not the same as a transit visa, which is legally obtained at borders for something like a train ride through a country. It is usually good for two or three days, long enough to pass through that country.

TRAVEL GUIDES AND INTERNET RESEARCH

For almost every country in the world, you can find a myriad of books and so-called travel guides claiming to be the most authoritative sources of information for that destination. It's even more amazing if you dig into the credentials of some of the authors of this travel pulp and realize they haven't lived the experiences they write about. Several people we've taken into Third World countries have read two or three hefty books and entered the trip with a preconceived idea of what they were going to encounter. They made the mistake of accepting the book as fact instead of what it is—the author's opinion relative to his individual perspective. A couple of these clients were even disappointed that the actual experience did not match what they had read in the book. They should have stayed home and been content with armchair traveling in the safe, controlled world of their living rooms.

The problem with most travel guides is that the research has been compiled from numerous sources instead of first-hand knowledge. It has been our experience that the areas we are always warned about are much more docile than they're portrayed. Many second-rate travel guides will scare you with horrific bullshit about visiting countries in revolution, then herd you into Rio de Janeiro or New Orleans during Carnival or Mardi Gras, havens for every type of trash and crook who infest the Earth.

If you are looking for an expert travel guide on the Third World, then choose one by an author who has the credentials and the in-the-trench time to back it up. Robert Young Pelton's *The World's Most Dangerous Places* is light-years ahead of the famous *Lonely Planet* guides when it comes to reality-based traveling in the Third World and dangerous places, which is probably the reason it's required reading by CIA personnel who travel to these regions.

Remember, no matter what you read about your destination country, your experience there may be totally different from someone else's. We go to these destinations because we don't know what we will find, which increases the adventure factor tenfold. We prepare as best we can for whatever will happen and draw our own conclusions based on our experiences. True adventure travel is a lot like learning to drive a car. Someone else can show you how a vehicle works, but it boils down to you getting behind the wheel and doing it yourself to fully understand how to drive.

If you plan to travel like this, then you may not need anything more than a small guide that provides only very basic information. One of the best examples of a basic travel guide is the *In Your Pocket* series that covers a lot of Central and East European cities and countries, including Russia, Lithuania, Belarus, Hungary, and Romania. Each *In Your Pocket* guide covers one city and country, has about 50 pages on soft paper, and will, as the name says, fit in your pocket. It contains basic information on everything from language and hotels to dentists and shoe repair, and it is researched and written by citizens of that country instead of some visiting traveler. You can even find the local hangout for prostitutes. The rest—the actual experiences—are left for you to encounter and learn from or not.

No matter which travel guide you rely on, always verify by phone or Internet research any information you intend to use from it. Many Third World countries have unstable commercial environments, so the hotel, museum, or money exchange rate you saw in a printed travel guide may not exist at the time of your visit.

The majority of research and preparation for any trip we take these days is done on the Internet and via e-mail. We research gear development, make airfare reservations, maintain client contact, search out those who have traveled the area, and stay informed about on-the-ground situations where we are going. Besides common sense, the Internet has probably done more to minimize risk in travel to the Third World than anything else in the last 50 years. Its single most important asset in this area is its ability to deliver current information. What happened an hour ago in Belarus or Colombia is at your fingertips, right down to the current temperature. It also can deliver an overwhelming amount of information, so it is up to you to sift through it and find what you need. Just be careful about believing everything you find, because good research means separating fact from bullshit.

CHAPTER 2

Preparing to Leave the Comforts of Home

Once you leave the comforts of home, especially if you're a first-time traveler, everything you've known about day-to-day life changes. You are stepping into a world of new languages and customs and possibly new dangers. If you think you have butterflies in your stomach just preparing for it, wait until your feet hit the ground.

Traveling into the Third World can be an intimidating experience if you allow it to be, but once you get acclimatized and moving around the landscape, you'll be glad you made the choice to visit such an exotic location. The secret to having an enjoyable learning experience is to relax, take things as they come, and remember: You're not in Kansas anymore.

GROUP VS. SOLO TRAVEL

When traveling solo, any potential risks to adventure travel go up considerably, so do all of your research and homework carefully. You may not attract as much attention as a big tour group, but being a lone target, you are generally considered easier prey for the bad guys. This makes it even more important not to wear the fluorescent tourist attire or five pounds of pierced body jewelry or generally look like the new circus in town.

If you decide to travel alone, you have to stay sharp, be aware of what's going on around you at all times, and have a good deal of self-confidence. You also have to do all your own legwork and rely only on your financial resources. If you get sick or win a stay in the local jail, you have no friends to help out. Here's a real good tip for solo travelers: Find a local you feel you can trust and keep feeding him dollars so he will be there to help you in a jam. This can be done by befriending him as a guide or consultant so you feel you're getting your money's worth.

The bright side to solo travel is that you have only yourself to worry about, which brings a great deal of freedom with it. It also teaches you to rely on yourself and forces you to

Traveling with a group is the safest way to go when exploring
harsh wilderness areas such as flooded lowland jungle.

learn more about the host country, thus building a ton of self-
confidence. Solo travel is also the way to go if you're trying to
avoid a lot of notice and need to achieve specific objectives.

Traveling with a companion or in a group solves a lot of
the woes of solo travel, but it is not without its own problems. Now you have to keep up with everyone's where-
abouts, worry about how their conduct may affect you and
the rest of the group, and deal with the more difficult logistics of travel arrangements for many rather than one. It has
its advantages too: Traveling in a large group may incur

greater expenses for some things like a bigger boat or plane for in-country travel, but you can usually get a cheaper per-person cost on other things like guide fees. For these reasons, a group should have at least one seasoned traveler on board who knows how to negotiate with the locals and deal with problems that may crop up.

In our adventure travel business, we make it a well-understood policy on the front end that one person will not ruin the trip for all. Idiots get shipped home real quick, and the rest of us continue on with the trip. This policy helps a great deal to keep people's behavior straight and pleasant. As a private traveler you will not have the luxury to take such drastic measures, so the bottom line is to choose your traveling companions very carefully. This is especially true when visiting Third World countries, where even seasoned travelers can become unglued.

All in all, it is usually safer to travel in groups. "There is strength in numbers" applies well here when it comes to protecting yourself from scam artists and bandits. Plus, you've got several folks' resources to fall back on in a crisis, and your friends can call your family if something happens to you.

If you choose to travel with a group, never use it as an excuse to be lazy when it comes to pulling your share of the load. In most groups there will be some who will use the energetic nature of other members as a crutch. Instead of doing things for themselves, they will sit back and allow the rest of the group to take care of them. It's fine to have people around you that you can count on, but when adventure traveling, always be as self-sufficient as possible since it makes life easier for the whole team.

PACKING FOR THE TRIP

Part of your destination research should be on what type of gear and clothing you will need once you're in-country. The climate and activities will dictate what you will need to bring, but in general most folks overpack, especially if it's their first time on this type of a excursion. Our advice is simple: When you leave home, leave home. Don't try to take it with you on your trip.

Remember one thing when packing: You will have to haul your stuff around wherever you go. You'll have to drag it through airports, on taxis, and through all types of Third World towns and cities, and during all of this you will be the only person responsible for keeping an eye on your stuff. It will get tiresome if you have a garbage can-sized duffel bag plus a couple of smaller bags.

Each time we go on a trip we end up taking less and less. We've learned that many things like extra clothes can be bought in-country, and we tend to give a lot of it away before leaving. You should be able to fit all of your clothes, gear, and personal items into one medium or large backpack and a small carry-on bag.

A good tip is to buy standard military dog tags with all your information printed on them and permanently attach them to your main bags. This saves a lot of time because you will no longer have to fill out those paper tags the airlines give you. Dog tags can be purchased from any major military surplus gear supplier such as Brigade Quartermasters (see the Acknowledgment and Resources section at the end of this book for contact information).

Your passport, visa, immigration papers, and money should be kept in a pouch hanging around your neck or on your person somehow. Your small carry-on bag and/or travel vest (more on these later) should hold personal hygiene items, camera, ink pen, personal survival kit, and any medication you are taking. This way you don't have to dig through your main pack to get to any items you may need on short notice. Any medication should be in the pharmacy container with the label that includes both yours and the doctor's name. Don't try to conserve space by putting medication in a smaller container or mixing it up in a zip-lock plastic bag. You may know what it is, but you'll

The authors have found lightweight travel vests to be the absolute best method for keeping important survival gear with them at all times.

never convince the police or customs officials that the bag of pills is legal.

If you plan on shooting a lot of pictures, take a lot of film. The overall quality of film available in Third World countries is generally not good. They may have name brands, but it will usually be way out of date or stored in very hot temperatures, which deteriorates the film quickly. Poor-quality developing fluids and cheap photo paper are also common in the Third World, so wait until you get home to have film developed. As far as packing film for travel through airport X-ray machines, don't worry about it if it's below 1000 ASA speed. We've shot tens of thousands of photos for magazine assignments overseas and we've never protected the film from X-ray, yet the developing has always worked out fine. If you're worried, you can either buy overpriced lead-lined film bags or ask that your film be inspected by hand instead of X-ray. Some airport security officers will not comply with this request, however, especially in the wake of September 11.

You can always find someone to do laundry even in the most remote places, so pack light on clothes. It should go without saying that you should match your clothes to the climate you will be in, yet we've seen people bring long underwear to the jungle! It is true that hot places are not always hot (and cold places can heat up pretty good in daylight hours), but maybe all you will need to knock the chill off in the wee hours of a jungle night is a long-sleeved shirt or rain poncho instead of long underwear and a down sleeping bag.

Leave your loud clothes, logo tee shirts, faddish styles, and body jewelry at home unless it happens to be the local dress where you are going. Dress neat and clean in cities but not expensive or loud. In general, don't dress like you are visiting; dress like you live there. Just don't go overboard and strut around like Lawrence of Arabia. You'll only look like a fool if you don't have the language skills and cultural knowledge to back it up. And wearing indigenous garb will not change the fact that no matter how much you dress down, you will always be considered a wealthy tourist to these people. Even if you are a college student who had to scrimp and save for the trip, the fact that you could afford a plane ticket overseas—not to mention attend college— automatically puts you in a privileged category in the eyes of the locals.

Take a lesson from a business associate of ours who operates in China, Russia, and other areas of political turmoil. Before he leaves home, he arranges to have his contacts pick him up at the airport in an old car so he doesn't look important. He knows that hanging around airports wearing expensive business suits and traveling via luxurious means would make him a bigger target for would-be kidnappers and scam artists. You should adopt the same philosophy. The key here is to appear to be obscure and unimportant. (You're going to hear this advice again and again throughout this book.)

Once you figure out what you need to pack, then you should give thought to how to pack it. There are two considerations here: in what order will you need the packed items, and how do you hide things that might prove too tempting for baggage handlers and other transportation workers?

Common sense should dictate the order in which you will need things, but a case of nervousness in a strange land can sometimes send common sense out to lunch. Always put things back in the same place when removing and replacing them in packs or luggage so you'll know where they are in the event you need them quickly. If your trip consists of different gear for different places, compartmentalize everything so you're not digging through tents to get to a clean shirt for dinner at a nice restaurant. In other words, store the same type of gear in the same pocket so you will instantly know where something is located throughout the trip. Stuff sacks and large zip-lock plastic bags are useful for compartmentalizing items in the main storage areas of your pack.

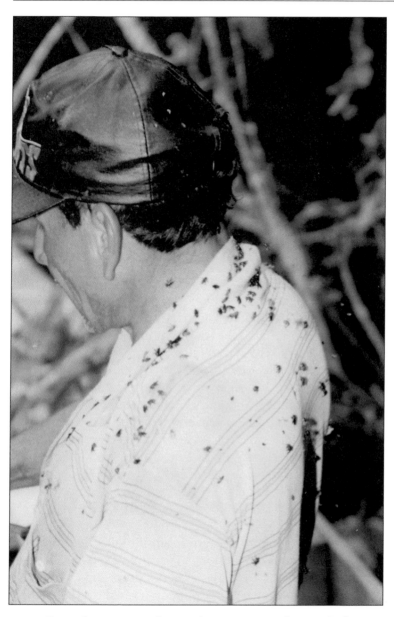

Always focus your packing on the requirements for your final destination. Forgetting simple items such as bug repellent in a tropical wilderness will make for a frustrating adventure.

Any liquids or chemicals such as liquor or bug repellent should be packaged to avoid spilling, then sealed securely inside a zip-lock bag. Airlines will not take luggage that obviously contains chemicals or has strange smells radiating from it.

Keep your camera, personal survival kit, and similar necessities with you at all times in a smaller bag or travel vest. Without exception, your documents and money are always kept securely on your person.

Certain valuables or expensive pieces of larger gear can be hidden in a wad of dirty clothes, a rolled-up tent, or other items stored toward the center of your pack or checked luggage. This might prevent the errant baggage handler from swiping something at the airport or bus station. If at all possible, keep smaller valuables on your person. The only exceptions to this are knives and other items that may not be legally taken aboard a plane in your carry-on luggage. Those will have to go into your checked baggage.

If you've purchased a nice souvenir, you might want to go to the nearest city and ship it home via FedEx or UPS rather than haul it around and worry about it being lost, stolen, or broken. Just make sure it's legal to export/import. For example, many shops in Latin America illegally sell jaguar paws and furs to unsuspecting tourists. Similarly, some woods that are used in carved souvenirs are illegal, even in souvenir form, to take out of the country or export into another country.

SCHEDULING YOUR TRAVELS

We once traveled to a remote mountain village in the middle of a very contentious upcoming election. Pickup trucks cruised the narrow streets, politicians bellowed through megaphones, and campaign workers threw cigarettes to the crowds. Military parades and out-of-tune brass bands took turns filling the town's main square when the candidates weren't shouting promises. It was Third World politics at its finest. Standing on the main plaza watching one speaker work the large crowd into a serious frenzy, we realized how dangerous this situation could be for a visitor from another country. If the speaker wanted to, he could have easily turned the crowd into an angry mob and against anyone he wished.

Although this type of Third World emotion is fun to witness, it can also turn deadly very suddenly, so consider all the angles when you schedule the time for your travels. Obvious factors such as weather and seasonal changes as well as the political climate can all be readily monitored via the Internet and news reports from your target area. As noted, it may not be best to visit in the midst of elections or political turmoil unless you're there for that reason. Be aware that during any big event or election, the cost of travel and lodging will increase dramatically. Plane and taxi fares can easily double and triple, and you may find no lodging at all.

You can make your own arrangements or ask a travel agent to arrange airfare for you. We suggest the latter because it gives you a level of protection for getting money refunded if something goes wrong. Whatever you do, make sure all international and in-country air travel is reserved *and* confirmed before you leave home, and be sure to leave plenty of layover time between flights. In the post-September 11 era we're living in, it's not uncommon for airlines to have serious delays or cancel flights altogether.

It's also wise to schedule a day layover in the city you'll be flying out of on your return trip home. If all flights are on time, then you'll have a day to organize your baggage and see a few sights. If flights are not going out on schedule, you'll be one of the first in line to catch the next available plane back to the States or your home country.

Whether you use a travel agent or you find airfare yourself, you should have paper tickets in your hand before you leave your home. This is true even if you are going with a tour guide who's meeting you at the airport. If someone else is making lodging arrangements for you, it doesn't hurt to call the hotel yourself and confirm reservations.

A popular option for travel these days is to get an electronic ticket (or "e-ticket") from the airline, where they simply issue you a confirmation number and you pick up your ticket and boarding pass when you check in. In our opinion, requesting a legal paper ticket eliminates the potential for one more screw-up by the airline. Although we have used e-tickets on many occasions, they add an unnecessary level of tension for the first-time traveler who walks into an airport, alone, without a ticket in his hand. A paper ticket is tangible and gives the newcomer more peace of mind.

PRE-TRIP EMERGENCY PLANNING

If there is one thing adventure travelers consistently fail to do, it is to plan for the unplanned. Most people arrange every detail of their excursion into the Third World boonies but, incredibly, never have a "bug-out plan" if things go wrong. This is natural since most people don't want to think of the nasty things that could happen on their vacation, or they believe it can never happen to them. Adopt the attitude that anything that can go wrong probably will, then plan accordingly.

A bug-out plan is simply an emergency plan to get help and/or get out in a crisis. Take the time to look at a map and see where you will be during your travels. This will give you at least a general idea of where cities, rivers, railroads, and roads are located if you need to get help. Find out where the embassy and the police stations are located in the cities. Think about what you absolutely have to have to survive, who you would contact, and how you would get home quickly in an emergency.

Your passport, visa, and immigration papers should stay on your person at all times. Also remember to keep copies of credit cards and contact information for the cards on your person, and have extra copies at home. Have a photocopy of your passport along with emergency contact phone numbers in a secure place in your pack. Keep emergency cash hidden on you, and don't reveal it in public.

We have a couple of friends, Curtis and Brian, who travel regularly to Honduras working on a project for indigenous people. Most of their work keeps them within the confines of remote areas, but a few years ago an incident occurred that changed their ideas on trip preparation.

After finishing a tour in the boonies, they decided to go into the city of La Ceiba for a good meal and some R&R before catching their flight back to the States. After arriving in town they stopped at a café for a bite, parking their Honduran government vehicle along the curb in broad daylight. Their passports, airline tickets, all their gear, and most of their cash was left in the car. They also left a camera sitting up on the dash in plain view. To complete the set of variables for this soon-to-be-learned lesson, there happened to be a big festival in town, which brought in every con artist and thief from every corner of Honduras to ply their trade.

Brian and Curtis had been in the café for only a few minutes when they went back to the car to retrieve a clean shirt. They immediately noticed that someone had neatly unlocked the car, removed most of the contents, then coolly locked it back up before they left. It turned out no self-respecting thief would be without keys to every government-owned Land Cruiser in the country!

Brian's passport, airline ticket, credit card, and some cash were in a small black briefcase that was camouflaged in the black interior of the car, so the thief missed it. Curtis, on the other hand, was now a vagabond.

U.S. Embassy personnel required either an old passport or a certified birth certificate for identification to apply for a new passport—no photocopies of anything would be accepted (which Curtis didn't have anyway). His wife FedExed an old passport to Honduras, and he had a photo taken in-country. After some light interrogation at the embassy (they wanted to make sure he hadn't run short on cash and sold his passport on the street), he was allowed to apply for a new one. He had it a week later, and Brian bought him a new airline ticket on the credit card that had been left in the briefcase.

In contrast to Curtis' ordeal, we know of an incident where someone walked into the embassy with nothing more than a driver's license and was allowed to apply for a new passport. After hearing both of these stories, we made numerous phone calls to various agents in Passport Services of the U.S. State Department to get an answer to this question: If your passport and all you own is lost or stolen overseas, how does one prove identity and citizenship, given the reasonable assumption that you wouldn't have a certified birth certificate or an old passport on you to apply for a new one?

All of my questioning to various polite government agents yielded this insightful answer: "Ummm, let me refer you to . . . ." One lady confidently stated the embassy would issue a "temporary" passport to get home on, good for one year. The Passport Legal Department, however, had never heard of such a document. Every person we talked with passed the buck until we finally arrived at two separate answering machines inside the Overseas Passport Services office. (By the way, Marionette and Sandra, we're still waiting on an answer to our voice mail messages.)

Here's the best you can do in a scenario involving a lost or stolen passport. Before you leave home, get a certified copy of your birth certificate, two passport photos, and a government-issued photo ID such as a driver's license. It couldn't hurt to have an extra photocopy of your passport in case you manage to lose that too. Put it all in a FedEx mailer and leave it with someone you can trust *and can reach* in an emergency. They'll be able to send it to you if you are relieved of your passport. Hopefully this same person can also be trusted enough to wire some money to you. Do not have them mail cash or credit cards—wiring money is quicker, safer, and more efficient.

When you walk into the embassy to report a lost or

stolen passport, expect a few frowns from the personnel because you were stupid enough to give everything you had to the guy holding a knife to your throat. Get a police report from the local law before you go to the embassy or they might ask you to go do that, then come back. The photocopy of your passport, if you still have it, will be welcome by the embassy but not as proof of identification. They will enter the number of the stolen passport into their computer system to flag it at ports of entry so anyone attempting to use it can be nailed.

What about the guy who supposedly got by with only a driver's license? Well, to the credit of some embassy personnel, there is a bit of "on the ground" discretion when it comes to these matters. Remember the golden rule: Be polite and smile, even when dealing with your own government. If you stay cool, calm, and honest, you'll get a lot more help from most folks than if you go in making demands. Apparently, some embassy personnel really believe they are there to help U.S. citizens in a crisis, even though they are not legally required to do so.

It turns out that the consular officer at the embassy *does* have the authority to issue you a temporary travel passport, good for three months, as long as he/she is satisfied as to your credibility. Spare documentation will greatly speed this process up, but it can be done with nothing more than a verbal interview. This is where a smile and being polite will pay off. Unless the consular officer thinks fraud might be involved, a police report is not mandatory in such cases, nor is any hard documentation as to your identity. You can read this on the U.S. State Department's Web site under "Lost and Stolen Passports Abroad" at http://travel.state.gov/lost_passports_abroad.html. (Thanks to the folks at EmbassyWeb.com for helping me finally mine this information out.)

Of course, the most important thing in any emergency is to stay calm and think. If you panic you can't think. Then you run the risk of becoming a victim of the closest con artist or thief.

TRAVEL SURVIVAL KITS

Travel survival kits are not full-blown survival kits such as those we carry during wilderness outings. They are simply compact bags that provide us with the bare essentials to survive short-term in any environment, urban or remote. The idea is that if your luggage is lost or stolen, you can live off the items in your kit for a few days. Anything else you can pick up at the nearest town with the money you were smart enough to keep on you.

A small travel survival kit should basically consist of the following: medication you may be taking, extra glasses if you wear them, first-aid gear, personal hygiene items, an ink pen, small flashlight, and several outdoor and miscellaneous survival tools which will be discussed in detail in Chapter 8. There are many such commercial travel kits on the market, and these are fine as long as they are small and easy to carry on the airplane.

As airline security becomes tighter and tighter, it becomes increasingly difficult to carry a decent travel survival kit on board an airplane. Simple survival items like a small knife or any sharp-edged tool are banned from carry-on baggage, and that is exactly where the survival kit should be—with you at all times.

A long time ago we got into the habit of using our carry-on bag as our travel survival kit. It's usually a large camera/utility bag containing camera equipment, documents, and some wilderness survival items. These personal kits keep you mobile and self-sufficient no matter what happens, so make use of them from the time you leave your home until you return. Typically we transfer our essential survival items to a more convenient travel vest for bush travel. Passports and vital documentation are always stored in a waterproof pouch and/or container throughout the trip.

CHAPTER 3

Arriving in the
Host Country

For first-time travelers, the initial adrenaline rush will be arriving on foreign soil, especially if you don't speak the native language.

I'll never forget my first trip outside my home country. My guide, who lived in the United States, was a seasoned wilderness professional but spoke absolutely none of the native language of our destination country. We were taking an extended excursion into the backcountry, so naturally large knives were a major part of our gear. Sensing my anxiety, customs officials began dumping all my bags and inspecting my belongings while asking questions in their native tongue with serious looks on their faces. I was alone and scared in a foreign country everyone had advised me not to visit. It felt as if the world was crashing down around me simply because I did not understand and was afraid I had violated their laws out of ignorance. My imagination quickly took control of my common sense, and all I could think about was spending the rest of my life in some rat-infested Third World jail. Eventually someone arrived who spoke English, and the matter was resolved and my nerves calmed.

Fear is the body's radar, piercing the unknown to retrieve signals. Just like radar it does not discriminate, leaving interpretation and reaction solely up to the brains of the system. While radar uses sophisticated circuitry and radio waves to do its job, fear uses adrenaline and, for lack of a better term, a sixth sense to perform its duties. Fear, when understood, is an asset to be harnessed instead of shunned—in other words, a valuable survival tool. Any person who claims he has no fear is either a fool or a liar, and from our experience it has always been the latter.

This chapter will inform the first-time adventurer of the fears, dangers, and unknowns of entering new worlds. Regardless of the itinerary, every overseas traveler will have to officially enter the country, change money, and acquire transportation before they can settle down and enjoy the ultimate goal of their adventure. Just remember that getting there is half the fun. Facing fears and conquering hurdles is the motivating factor behind every hard-core adventurer. Learning to act calmly instead of react irrationally places you in control of your own destiny, even when the chips are down and things look grim.

LUGGAGE SECURITY

"Never leave your baggage unattended." You've heard this a thousand times if you've frequented airports. Live by it when in any airport, domestic or foreign. Leaving your pack or bag unattended is virtually guaranteed to invite theft or leave you open as an unsuspecting "mule" for smugglers. It literally takes a split second for someone to pick up a bag from your side while your head is turned the other way. Put a leg through a strap, sit on it, or attach it somehow to your body, but stay with it. If it becomes necessary for you to leave your bags, find a short-term baggage storage service within the airport. Make sure you get a receipt that notes the exact number of bags you have stored in their lockers.

Before you check your bags at the ticket desk, secure all loose straps and other dangling parts to the main body of the bag. This is very important because large international airports use conveyor systems to get the baggage to your plane. If the strap gets hung up or caught on a piece of equipment, it may not get on your flight. Packs can also be placed inside a duffel bag to prevent their straps from getting hung up. In Third World airports, once bags are checked it is usually easy enough to watch them go on the wagon and onto the plane and come off and into the terminal on the other end.

If you find something missing from your luggage, report it to airport officials. You probably won't get the missing item back, but insist on a written report because your insurance policy might require this documentation before it will replace the cost.

For added peace of mind on checked luggage, you can lock it or put it inside a padlocked duffel bag. There are two trains of thought here. Obviously, a lock can help deter theft of items inside the luggage as well as prevent a smuggler from slipping something into your bag. If an official wants to search it, he will find you and ask you to unlock it. No big deal. The other side of this is that a big fat padlock might make folks think there is something valuable inside your duffel, thus drawing unwanted attention to it. If the thief is really determined he might simply slit the bag with a knife and go fishing with his hand anyway. Another problem with locks is losing the keys, which makes for a nerve-racking experience when the military-looking official with a stern face wants you to unlock your bag.

If someone asks me whether to lock luggage, I generally say yes just in the interest of taking every reasonable precaution to prevent problems. However, we don't always lock ours simply because we don't put anything in the pack or duffel we can't afford to lose. Besides, it's a real bitch fumbling with keys when you need to open the bag.

When you arrive in-country, be wary of independent porters working for tips. Many times they will scoop your bags up without asking if you need help. They may appear helpful at first, then argue when you offer them an honest tip. Negotiate and settle on a price before you hire any such assistance at the airport or anywhere else.

Finally, *never* take or hold a bag or the belongings of anyone you don't know real well. This advice holds true not only for strangers but also for people in your travel group who you may have only known for a little while. If the bag happens to contain drugs, explosives, or anything illegal, you'll have a great deal of explaining to do and will probably be arrested.

Keep in mind that some Third World airports have little or no security when it comes to baggage. This is especially true of in-country flights between smaller cities. That means no metal detectors, no dogs, and rarely a bag search, so it may be highly likely that contraband material could come in close contact with you. So we say it again: Don't take possession of anything from anyone you don't know.

IMMIGRATIONS AND CUSTOMS

Although Customs and Immigrations can be an intimidating experience, for the most part as long as you are polite, keep a smile on your face, and have your papers in order, you will be able to breeze through without much of a delay.

Research your destination to make sure you are not violating any laws by bringing in contraband goods. What may be legal in the United States may not be legal in a foreign country. This could include things as seemingly innocuous as certain types of electronic equipment and printed material (especially true for Communist and certain Muslim countries).

Also be sure to check visa requirements through the U.S. State Department and secure all necessary visas before departing. Most airlines in the United States will not give you a boarding pass if you do not have a valid passport and correct visas for your final destination. The definition for "final destination" in airline lingo is the final place you are going on their airline or partner airline. Your actual final destination may vary due to overland travel across borders or in-country flights, so be sure to check every aspect of entry requirements for your entire itinerary.

These are only general rules, and some hard-core adventurers have been known to not play by the rules. A friend of ours, Bill Johnson, was so intent on fighting communism and leading an adventurous lifestyle that he dropped out of medical school to travel the world. With only a stint in ROTC as his military experience, he traveled to Afghanistan determined to volunteer for the Afghan *muzhedin* and take part in their fight against the Soviets. After trying to enter the country in several places, he found himself imprisoned in Pakistan for an illegal border cross-ing. After his short stay as a guest of the Pakistani govern-ment, he eventually made it into Afghanistan. The lesson? Persistence does pay off, but always be careful in your methodology.

When entering any country, one of the most important pieces of travel gear you will need is a pen. I can't recall the number of times I've stood in Immigration lines watching travelers go into a panic trying to find a pen. During the flight they forgot about completing their Customs and Immigration forms and were forced to turn to fellow travelers to help them.

Two rules of surviving travel have been violated here. The first is obvious laziness on the traveler's part by not tak-ing care of the small issues when they arise. In most situa-tions you will be given Customs and Immigrations papers during your flight. Fill these out as soon as you get them, then store them with your passport in your secure storage pouch. In general, you should never procrastinate on issues that concern your status as a foreign visitor. Taking care of paperwork as soon as you can gives you time to resolve any questions or concerns while surrounded by people who can help in your native language.

The second violated rule is relying on other travelers to supply you with tools to complete your journey. Although there will always be circumstances that will dictate accept-ing assistance from other travelers, try to be as self-sufficient as possible. This means planning ahead. Asking for help on issues that could easily have been handled yourself makes you appear weak in the eyes of those who would take advantage of you. Also consider that once you get to a point of panic, such as those folks who forgot about their Immigrations papers, then your mind is not free to focus on your surroundings. The fallout from this can vary from mis-placing your personal belongings to losing your passport and papers. Be aware at all times, and don't allow the little things to distract you. Even if you do forget something, just remain calm and work it out as you go.

Once you reach the Immigrations officer, don't try to impress him with the three new words of native language you learned on the plane. He may think you know the language and try to ask more questions than necessary. Most of the time, playing dumb with a friendly face gets you a lot further than trying to be intelligent. Appearing unimportant is the best route to take during 90 percent of your travel.

(There are rare times when making yourself appear more important than you are can be beneficial. For example, during one trip to a Latin American country, I was asked a lot of questions by an Immigrations officer—more than I usually get asked when going through the line. I could tell he was just giving me a hard time, so I pulled out a business card of a colonel in his military and told him I was in his country to do business with this man, which was true. The officer immediately stamped my passport and said in English, "Have a good day, sir.")

When dealing with Immigrations, it's usually best to wait in line patiently, have your papers in order, and give them to the officer when it's your turn. If questions are asked that you don't understand, respond with a calm voice in your native language, "I don't understand." The officer will either get a translator or just allow you to go on if he feels translation is more trouble than it's worth. Whatever you do, do not nod in agreement or answer any question you do not understand or think you understand.

In some countries the Immigrations officer will give you a slip of paper that verifies you are a legal and registered visitor of the country. This should be stored with your passport. During one of our jungle survival trips in Peru, one of our clients failed to secure his immigration papers properly. Two weeks later he went through the National Police line to board his plane for the United States and was stopped. After much delay and stern lectures from the police he was allowed to proceed, but only after paying a hefty fine. By now his papers have undoubtedly rotted away in the Amazon jungle somewhere.

One important note that needs to be added here is about how you store your passport and important papers. Never store these documents in your carry-on luggage while on the plane. There are a couple for reasons for this. The obvious one is to prevent them from being stolen, but the other is in case of quick evacuation. When I was on the plane that had the bombing attempt against it, we were forced off the plane quickly via the safety slides and were not given time to retrieve any carry-on luggage. Luckily, I had cash and all my papers with me. During our six-hour delay I was able to buy food and move about freely while other passengers were relegated to a confined area.

Next to your health, your passport is your single most important possession when traveling abroad. Buy a waterproof neck pouch that fits inside your shirt or one designed specifically for secure inside-the-pants carry and store your passport, immigration papers, airline tickets, baggage claim tickets, airport parking ticket, some cash, and all other important documents inside. Most important of all, never allow it to leave your person. Anytime you remove something from the pouch, always place it back when you're finished. During the numerous expeditions we have guided, we have witnessed horror stories with lost documents ranging from clients leaving their passports inside returned rental cars to having passports fall out of their back pockets when walking down a crowded street.

Perhaps one of the funniest incidents involved a doctor we had as a client on a trip to South America. He actually lost his boarding pass as soon as it was issued to him in Miami. He freaked out in line waiting to get on the plane and strip-searched himself. We managed to talk the airline into letting him board without his boarding pass, and he later found it when we arrived at our destination. It was in his shirt pocket.

Again, panic and losing control of your ability to think will cause you to overlook even the most obvious things. If you are too absentminded to take care of your stuff, then ask a friend or a trusted guide to secure them for you. Just remember, there may be times when you are alone and need your possessions, so carefully consider this option before relying on it.

After completing the relatively simple task of passing through Immigrations, you will move on to Customs, where you will claim checked baggage, declare certain items, and pay taxes on these goods if required. For most recreational travelers there will be no items that need declaring, but always research your country before assuming this. Communist and Muslim countries may have a surprisingly long list of items that require declaration, so read the instructions on the back of the form carefully before automatically stating you have nothing to declare.

Depending on the country you are visiting, your bags may arrive in Customs on a baggage claim belt or be thrown in a pile on the floor. This is usually very chaotic because every tired traveler is itching to get their stuff and be on their way. Don't become impatient, and most of all stay aware. When traveling in a group, designate at least one trusted person to watch all the carry-on luggage while the rest of the group goes to claim all the baggage. (Two is even better, as one person would have his hands full with even an obvious attempt to distract him.) Once all bags have been accounted for, move up to the Customs line together and proceed with only your bags. Once you clear Customs, you will not be allowed back inside if another person in your group gets pulled for inspection, so maintain control of your own baggage until you are cleared.

Getting inspected at Customs is usually a crapshoot. In a few of the countries we have visited, tourists press a button after giving the officer their Customs forms. These electronic devices generate random search/don't search instructions. If you are green-lighted, then you proceed without being searched. If you are red-lighted, then you move to an inspector's line for a routine search of your baggage.

Other countries may choose to "100 percent," which is

Customs talk for checking everyone on the plane. You will see this a lot when returning to the United States from countries known to be sources of drug smuggling. When 100-percent checks are done, most of the time the bags are passed through a type of X-ray machine, which is less time-consuming than physical searches by inspectors.

You may also be pulled for inspection randomly by officers trained to recognize suspicious behavior. If you are dressed in gang attire showing off your "colors" or just enjoy being obnoxious, then you increase your chances of being inspected. No matter what politically correct government agents say, they *do* use profiling when deciding to inspect an individual. So forget about your civil rights because the ACLU is not going to help you when you're in Customs territory—and that *includes* when you're in the United States border areas.

True story: A federal agent we know was assigned to question suspicious travelers on their way to a known drug-smuggling country. In law-enforcement slang terms they were looking for "smurfs"—people who smuggle large sums of money to pay for contraband items. The agent noticed a beautiful woman standing in line wearing a short skirt and decided to question her just because he found her attractive. Although he had no suspicion that she was violating any law, his training picked up on her nervous reaction to his request. Upon further investigation, he found that she and her boyfriend were carrying more than $50,000 in unreported cash. The simple fact of looking good and dressing sexy resulted in her being charged with smuggling and the loss of the money. The moral to this story: Always try to appear as unimportant as possible to avoid standing out in a crowd.

If you are pulled aside for questioning or inspection, the best advice is to not get nervous. The process can range from a quick once-over to an all-out search of everything, so just be polite and follow instructions. As long as you have done your research on legalities, followed those guidelines, and maintained control of your bags, there should be no problems.

Only in the most suspicious cases will Customs do what is known as a "secondary." This usually involves being taken into a special room to be interviewed, and yes, this could possibly lead to the legendary full-body search. Having worked around law enforcement for years, I am constantly amazed at the lengths to which people will go to conceal illegal items, from stashing condom-encased narcotics up their butts to shipping a crudely packed crate of M16s in a box marked "housewares" through one of the heaviest-watched ports in the United States.

If you are traveling legally with no ill intent, then clearing the officials is the easiest part. Again, the bottom line is to be honest, remain polite, don't stand out in the crowd, don't initiate conversation with the officers, and, most important, always be legal. Most Third World countries are begging for tourism dollars and will usher tourists through expeditiously. Even the Communist country of Cuba welcomes American tourists and their cash with open arms and probably won't even stamp your passport so you don't have problems with U.S. officials on your return. (As of this writing, it was still technically illegal for an American citizen to travel to and spend money in Cuba without prior authorization from the U.S. State Department, although it is done all the time.)

BRIBING AND SMUGGLING AS SURVIVAL TOOLS

Having advised you of the proper methods to get through Immigration and Customs, the flip side is that there will always be crooks and shysters in every system, and it's possible that you may have to deal with some of them. The authors of this book do not participate in or condone any illegal activities. We strongly believe in and enforce the rules of staying legal and maintaining a good attitude when we are traveling abroad alone or with associates. However, we feel it is important to include a few tricks of the illicit trade here. The reason for this is simple: We've been to many countries that just don't play by the rules, and a survival situation could occur that demands using every means possible to get out alive. Bribing officials and smuggling items across borders should be used only as a last resort to survive. Very few things are immoral or illegal if it involves saving your own life.

If you feel your travels have taken a turn that leave no alternatives, then try one of these "ethical" ways to bribe a law-enforcement officer:

1) Always take extra of anything that might attract attention. If you are taking in expensive bottles of liquor, pack an extra one to offer as a "gift." We have done this many times with knives and gear. Our large knives usually attract Customs attention, so we always have a few giveaway pieces, typically given out of courtesy more than as a bribe.

2) Before departing for a Third World country, roll up twenty or thirty $1 bills and place them in your front pocket. Once you realize that an officer is shaking you down, reach in your pocket as if to grab your identification and allow the bills to fall on the ground. As you fumble around gathering up your money, ask the officer if you can just pay the fine for the alleged infraction. The thing that you need to remember when offering a gift like this is that you may have to bestow one on every officer there. To keep from having to pay off everyone with a uniform, try to deal with the highest-ranking official. The most important thing is to always make sure your offer is done in an honorable way so you don't embarrass the officer. Also remember that bribes typically only work in desperate countries where officials can't support their families on their small salaries.

If you are one of those individuals intent on smuggling items in or out of a country, then the first thing you must do is prepare yourself for the consequences of your actions.

If you transport drugs or other contraband into or out of a foreign
country, you will eventually get caught no matter who you are.

No matter who you are, you will eventually get caught, and the consequences are usually severe.

Many folks end up getting cold feet on their smuggling adventure and either ditch the goods before traveling or abandon their baggage when they see that Customs is pulling a 100-percent check at the border. With airport security the way it is now, this is very difficult to do because every bag is bar-coded and matched to the ticket holder. Any sort of nervous attitude or unusual behavior is easily recognizable and will lead to your demise. Customs agents are trained to recognize such behavior, and they monitor it closely with cameras, hidden observation rooms, and roving plainclothes agents appearing to be other tourists. They also operate off anonymous tips, many of which are unverified and do not come from certified informants. In other words, anyone who doesn't like you or wishes to delay your journey can easily do so by making a simple anonymous phone call. Even though providing such false information is often a crime, it can happen, so be careful of who you piss off whether you're a smuggler or an honest tourist just trying to get home.

Some of the best smugglers do their dirty deeds blatantly and in the open. One plan we heard about involved the transportation of a 40-pound pre-Colombian gold idol that was robbed from an Indian grave in Latin America. The smugglers planned to take the artifact out by sailboat, painting it white over a thin layer of plaster. The idol would then be secured at the stern of the boat as a "mascot." They believed that placing the piece in the open and giving it a weathered look would lessen the suspicion that it was actually worth millions of dollars. It was a nice plan, but it was scrapped after one of the smugglers had a dispute with his mistress and she informed the authorities of his operation. The idol was eventually sold by other means. Probably the most important lesson to be learned from this story is that, if you choose to participate in illegal activities, keep it to yourself and trust no one.

Another common smuggling technique is to get some clean-cut tourist to carry the goods across the border. This is done either directly by paying the "mule," as these people are known, or indirectly by stashing the goods in an unsuspecting person's pack and stealing it back once it clears Customs.

Another trick is to use decoys to lure dogs and human detectors away from the actual smuggler. Detection dogs sniff out contraband because they think it's fun. Even well-trained attack dogs don't bite because of meanness; they bite because they've been trained to recognize it as fun and know they will be rewarded. Detection dogs are no different. They enjoy their work and will typically key on even the smallest scent. Many smugglers use this training against the dogs by deploying scented decoys (known or unknown to the decoy) to create distractions so the dogs key on someone else, thus drawing attention away from those actually carrying the contraband.

This same process is also used against the human detectors. Typically, someone who is known to be associated with the wrong crowd is recruited to be on a specific flight or at a particular border crossing, and the attention becomes focused on this suspicious character who is not breaking the law while the real law breaker calmly slips past. The bottom line is that law enforcement is limited in its available manpower and thus its ability to inspect every person. To do this would basically shut down airports and drastically affect commerce. Smugglers use this to their advantage. Sometimes law enforcement gets lucky and catches the bad guys, but the amount of illegal drugs reaching American streets shows that many, many more slip through the cracks undetected.

The sad part about all of this is that law enforcement is so overburdened that it has gotten to the point where they don't even care about the small fish. During one of our return trips from Latin America, we were standing outside the Miami airport smoking a cigarette while waiting for our connecting flight home. As I went to put out my cigarette in an ashtray, I noticed a small vial of something that appeared to be crack cocaine (which I had learned to recognize from my law-enforcement experience). I immediately found a police officer, brought him over, and showed him what was in the ashtray. He commented, "Yep, we see that all the time," and walked off. When we left, the cocaine was still there. Basically the cop didn't give a shit and didn't care that it was still on the street just waiting for anyone to pick it up. In fact, he seemed to be pissed off that I even bothered him with such a trivial matter. This attitude is probably why honest citizens refuse to get involved or assist in stopping illegal contraband. Our advice to any traveler is to mind your own business and you won't end up pissing off the smugglers or the people paid to stop them.

We can't stress enough that being legal at all times is the best way to enjoy adventure travel. We do not condone smuggling, nor have we ever smuggled anything into or out of a foreign country. The only reason we touched on this subject is because survival has no bounds in a life-or-death situation. Having said that, I'm not even sure we could name an instance where smuggling would be required to secure your personal survival. If it came to that, then there are usually plenty of other ways to prolong your life, and they're much easier than trying to smuggle anything into or out of a country. Don't do it!

FOREIGN CURRENCY

Our experiences have proven that, next to an open mind and nonthreatening attitude, money is the number one survival tool of adventure travel. Without sufficient cash or other medium of exchange, the risks increase when traveling through dangerous places. If you place yourself in the position of having to beg for a job, a ride, a meal, or any other necessity of life, there will always be people ready to take advantage of your situation.

Some of the best adventure travel exists in countries that

suffer from an "economy of desperation" syndrome. In these countries, the economy is in shambles, jobs are scarce, and locals make their living by any means possible. These circumstances usually produce an array of honorable and dishonorable entrepreneurs in search of the American dollar.

Simply put, money is the fuel that powers the world, and even though we have met many giving people during our travels, charity will last only so long. Even during dire situations, you will eventually wear out your welcome when your lack of contribution begins to take food off your host's table. The gradual effects of tourists taking advantage of desperate economies have made many indigenous people slow to trust.

When traveling in strange lands, don't be a moocher, but at the same time don't be an easy mark for shysters. Pay your fair share and treat everyone with respect, but be firm when it comes to getting what you are paying for. As a last resort, always budget at least a 20-percent margin of extra cash for any unexpected "adventures" that arise, and whatever you do, be sure to keep the existence of this stash known *only* to yourself.

Just before you set out on your trip, check the currency exchange rate of the country or countries you plan to visit. Advertised rates will typically differ from actual rates in-country. This is determined by the fluctuating state of the economy and may change on a daily basis. When you arrive at the airport for departure, change a small amount of American dollars into foreign currency so you can pay for taxis, porters, or other services once you arrive at your destination, but do the rest of your exchanging once you are safely settled in overseas.

Why not just change it all while you're still in the United States or your home country? Simple answer: You will usually get a better rate for your dollar once you are in your destination country. For example, the current U.S. airport exchange rate for Peruvian *soles* is 2.7 *soles* for one dollar, but once you get into the country the rate is 3.45 *soles* to a dollar. As a general rule, countries with bad economies are a good bargain for travelers, and the exchange rate margin will grow as the country's economy declines.

Any American dollars you take into a foreign country should be clean, new bills. Since the design change of American paper money, foreign banks and money changers have become very leery of the old bills due to the potential for counterfeiting. If your bills are dirty, torn, or have marks that shouldn't be on them, then you may have a problem exchanging them overseas. Some street changers will take dirty bills but may give a lower return rate compared to crisp new bills. Also consider that many countries take dollars as a secondary currency, while others have laws against any American money, so fully research this before arriving at your destination. If you do choose to carry dollars as an exchange medium, be sure you have various smaller denominations because some businesses and locals may not be able to change large bills.

In countries with high crime rates, carry a small amount of money in a throwaway wallet kept in your pants pocket. It should contain various business cards and other papers to make it appear to be your primary money compartment. We also advise having a small amount of loose money in another pocket to pay for things such as food, drinks, and taxi fare. Keep the remainder of your cash in a secure place such as the neck or inside-the-pants pouch discussed earlier. Make all of your street transactions from either the throwaway wallet or the loose stuff in your pocket. Resupply cash to the wallet and your pocket in the safety of your hotel room or other private area.

Besides pickpocketing, probably the largest petty crime carried out against tourists is money-changing scams. Dishonest money changers have perfected the art of making off with tourists' money. Counterfeiting is easily perpetrated against those unfamiliar with the host country's currency, but one of the most common scams is a simple sleight-of-hand change. The changer will stuff paper in between bills, making the stack of unfolded money appear accurate, but it will actually contain several folded bills inside. When the changer counts the money in front of you, he will do so from the folded end and actually count several of the same bills twice since he is counting the folded bills. It looks good to you until you walk away and realize what has happened. At this point it's too late to prove anything, and you just have to live with what you received.

The simplest scam is to quote you one exchange rate but actually give you less. The changers do this through speed and confusion, playing on your trust and unfamiliarity with the local currency. If you change money, always have a calculator handy, know how much you should receive, and demand the changer hand count the bills one at a time into your hand.

Black market money changers are prominent in Third World countries. Be wary of those who insist on making the transaction out of the public eye—either he is doing his act against the law, or he has other devious plans such as mugging, robbing, or even kidnapping you. Always try to deal with people who do their deed in front of God and everyone else and you will be much better off. If for some reason you must use a shady money changer, then always take a companion to watch your back during the deal.

Your best bet for changing money is a bank or other official money-changing location. If these are an option, always take the extra time to use them because street changers may be illegal in some areas. Banks may ask you to produce your passport before you can initiate an exchange, and some may require a second government-issue photo ID (as in Vietnam, for example). Allow the clerk to see your passport, but never allow him or her to take it out of your sight. If they insist on making a copy of it or anything else that removes the document from your possession, then politely tell them you want to accompany it when they do so. If they do not agree with this, then retrieve your passport and find another location to change money.

Even when dealing with banks, always calculate the amount you should receive based on their advertised rate, and count the money in the presence of the person making the exchange. If it's a large sum of money, proceed to a nearby place of privacy to store your money in your primary pouch. Never shove it in your pocket or wallet since petty thieves keep an eye on tourists going in and out of banks. Pickpockets operate quickly and efficiently, using techniques from the old bump-and-extract method to slicing open your pocket with a razor blade to having gangs of local children surround you with offers to purchase trinkets while one of them rifles your pockets. There is no surefire safe method to carry money in your clothing, so always carry the bulk of it along with your other valuables in a separate pouch inside your clothing.

Many of our clients ask us about carrying travelers checks. As a general rule we don't recommend them for serious adventure travel. They're fine when you're in a larger city with access to banks, but if you rely on them in remote locations you will probably die of starvation. If you insist on carrying travelers checks, we suggest keeping them as the emergency 20-percent portion of your funds. If you decide to use them, be sure to only sign them on the bottom line in the presence of the clerk at the time of cashing. Presigning a check in both signature locations may be grounds for rejection by the clerk because it's hard to verify your signature otherwise, and it creates the possibility of fraud if the checks are stolen.

Credit cards are perhaps the greatest double-edged financial sword in the history of the world. Nowadays they're mandatory financial instruments for travelers, but they also open the door to all sorts of fraud and voluntary overspending. If you travel enough, credit cards will eventually play a role since they are sometimes required for renting cars and reserving hotels and plane tickets, but in our opinion they should be used as tools only and never viewed as cash.

The trick to successful adventure traveling is budgeting enough cash to make the trip flow but to always have an emergency financial plan, such as a credit card, when things turn bad. We prefer American Express because there is no preset spending limit. In an emergency situation, this would allow us to evacuate an entire team out of a country with upgraded plane fare if our regular tickets didn't work, then worry about paying the bill once we were safe at home. American Express also offers a range of travel insurance and in-country benefits should you become desperate. Some of these are unadvertised advantages such as quick action on billing disputes.

Several years ago we purchased airline tickets directly from a foreign airline for our team of adventurers. One week before departure the airline went bankrupt, leaving us holding $4,000 of worthless tickets. We immediately entered a billing dispute with American Express because we had purchased the tickets on their card. Amex credited our account for the full amount, and we purchased tickets through another airline and made the trip. If we had paid cash, we would have been left holding the bag for four grand.

Again, use credit cards as tools, but never think of them as free cash or try to rely on them as your primary means of finance overseas. There are many remote places where a credit card is useless, regardless of your excellent credit or financial status. Finally, always notify your card company of your planned trip with dates so they will be expecting charges from overseas.

INFRASTRUCTURE AND ENVIRONMENT

In the developed world we have at our disposal every conceivable form of transportation, from elevators to jumbo jets. Instantaneous communication around the globe is literally at our fingertips. The most advanced medical care is readily available, and garbage disposal is both a science and unionized industry. Our entire infrastructure is a carefully micromanaged web of connected dependency, developed to predict and control our world in order to eliminate surprise and uncertainty and to adjust to our needs and whims.

In Third World countries, the infrastructure works in harmony with, rather than trying to control, the environment. The concept of living in harmony with the environment is still in vogue, as it has been for several thousand years. Modern infrastructure is largely unknown, unavailable, and in many cases simply unwanted by remote people who wisely recognize that trying to control their environment with complicated infrastructures will ultimately lead to its destruction.

Remote villages in the Amazon jungle usually consist of fewer than 50 people. The system of many small villages dispersed over a large area has worked well in the jungle for several reasons. Whether the villagers are hunter-gatherers, farmers, or both, food is not depleted in any one area by a small group. Should a disease like malaria, dengue, or cholera break out, it will remain confined to a small number of people. The human waste and damage to the surrounding environment is minimal and easily absorbed by the jungle. All of their needs, from building shelter to acquiring food and water, are provided by the surrounding wilderness. They are in fact self-sufficient and rely on no outside support to thrive.

But this system creates a problem for outsiders who want consistent, easy access to these people. Many missionary groups that want to "save" the "savages" really don't want to trek around to a zillion small villages scattered throughout the jungle, so they try to entice the remote people to move to a larger river village with promises of modern amenities and a "better" life.

I remember standing on the bank of the Ucayali River looking at a modern village of about 500 people engineered by a missionary group. The running water was pumped from the river into a water tank in the village and gravity-fed to the houses. The pump was run by a diesel generator that also

A typical Third World suburb has sewage and
trash dumped directly into the river system.

provided electricity to the homes. But there was one major
problem: The community septic system emptied the effluent
into the river upstream from the water tower intake.

So now the formerly self-sufficient jungle people had
running water polluted by the septic system upstream and
a bill for the diesel-run electricity. (No, it wasn't provided to
them for free.) Because of the large number of people concentrated in one area, they had depleted game in the surrounding area and had become dependent on river trade for
some of their food. If sickness broke out, it affected 500
people instead of 50. And they received all of this for the

small price of giving up their old religion and becoming Christians. They are now like modern man, thoroughly dependent on others for their existence. What a nice "improvement" for the indigenous Amazonians.

Infrastructures in Third World countries are usually basic to primitive. It is up to you to leave your notions of comfort and convenience behind and adapt to the host country's conditions. In short, your success for an enjoyable trip depends on your attitude. Although it is possible to find an occasional oasis of modern comfort, it should not be expected.

Your expectations for infrastructure should be very basic. A toilet could be anything from what you have at home (minus the seat) to a funnel wired up in one corner of the bar you're in to simply nature's best—the bushes. If it's a regular bathroom, don't be surprised to find an attendant who will expect payment before letting you pass to answer the call of nature. We've had more than one client who drew back in anger shouting, "I'm not going to pay that kid 25 cents to take a piss!" It's how the kid makes money to put bread on the table, so pay him and go on.

Communication will be covered in detail later, but suffice to say here that some Third World cities have great telephone systems and in many cases better switching equipment than is found in some areas of the United States. We've traveled all over the world installing the latest digital telecommunications equipment in some of the nastiest dumps you can imagine, and I am amazed by the money being spent on this industry overseas. This is mainly due to foreign investments and a subsidized push to upgrade communications in the cities, but once you go remote you'll be lucky if there are any phones at all. Those you do find will be radio-phone patches that may or may not work. The guide you hired will assure you communication is great because you can go to the phone office in that small town and use the radio-phone. The only problem is that they require someone to be in attendance on both ends. The guy at the other end may be at siesta or flirting with the girl at the corner market while you are talking to dead air. It is best to simply assume they won't work and be pleasantly surprised if they do.

THIRD WORLD TRANSPORTATION

Probably about the most fun and fear you will experience in any single event of your traveling is using local transportation. In some Third World countries it's comparable only to surviving an out-of-control roller coaster—absolutely thrilling . . . after it's over. Looking back on our travels, our experiences on buses, cabs, ferries, and other forms of local transportation are without doubt the most dangerous trips we have ever taken.

Although some countries regulate public transportation, many do not. In these countries, anyone with anything that rolls or moves seems to be in the tourist transportation business. Every one of these people are always the "best guide in the whole country," according to themselves. From taxi drivers to tour operators, these people will offer you the world and even physically fight other operators to get a few of your American dollars.

Typically, your first encounter with this phenomenon will be when you exit the airport. Most of the time you will be greeted by a mob of folks shouting "Taxi!" They may not know another word of English, but this one word is usually spoken with a perfect American accent.

How you choose your driver may vary depending on where you are going, the number of people in your group, and how much gear is being hauled, but one rule of thumb should always be observed—negotiate and settle on the price *before* you enter the vehicle or even put your bags in the trunk. If you are traveling solo and are not sure about the area you will be traveling to, check with airport officials for opinions and recommendations of drivers and approximate rates.

Once you have hired your driver and are moving

toward your destination, make a mental map of your route through the city. More than one attempted heist has been foiled by the traveler understanding where he was and how to get back to where he came from. Make mental notes of safe zones where there are people and activity nearby. If you're traveling alone, try to sit behind the driver with clear access to a door that opens. Should you have to bail out in a hurry, forget about the luggage and get away from the situation only with the valuables you have on your person.

We have no special advice for the absolutely terrifying rides you may experience with Third World transportation. Speed limit markers, stop signs, and traffic lights are for decoration only. The driver will blare the horn constantly, and he will seemingly pay no heed to oncoming traffic, not to mention the hordes of pedestrians, motor scooters, bicycles, ox carts, donkeys, dogs, and chickens crowding the roads. Just when you think a crash is inevitable, someone will veer out of the way at the last moment, narrowly escaping collision. It's best described as a real-world, everyday game of chicken. All you can do is sit back, enjoy the ride, and try not to think about the bald tires and driver's lack of attention. Incredibly, there are very few accidents involving transportation of tourists.

On one of our trips, we had a team member suffer a serious panic attack while traveling over a dangerous mountain pass in a minivan. Suddenly we were in the middle of nowhere with a person who was way past the point of logic. There was nothing we could do to reason with him or convince him he was not going to die. All he wanted to do was get out of the vehicle and walk to the bottom, even though the bottom was 3,000 feet straight down. He finally calmed to the point where he agreed to make it to the top, but once there he did get out and hire a local guide to walk him down the other side. On a follow-up trip a couple of years later, he returned to the same mountain to conquer his fear. He made it to the top but once again walked down.

Bus travel is an adventure in itself. There's no such

thing as too many people or animals in, on, or under a Third World bus. If you decide to rely on the bus as your method of transportation, be prepared for absolute chaos once you arrive at the bus station. Maintain control of your gear and stay aware as you negotiate price and destination. Once you board, try to sit by a window on the same side where your luggage is loaded. Every time the bus stops, keep a sharp eye so your luggage is not "mistakenly" taken off the bus. Sitting beside the window also gives you an escape route on most large buses, allows you to control the air flow, and keeps at least one part of your body against a wall, providing a side to store your valuables away from the quick hands of thieves.

During one of our trips to the top of the Andes Mountains, we endured a grueling fourteen-hour ride on a typically overcrowded bus. Some of our team stood the whole way while the rest were jammed in like sardines, enduring hairpin turns, huge potholes, and the same Spanish music audio cassette playing at full volume for the duration of the journey. I was sitting beside a young Spanish girl who had severe motion sickness, and every turn in the road produced another load of vomit soaking into my pants and shoes. After we arrived at our destination, the driver opened the cargo hold and two dust-covered stowaways crawled from the top of the luggage, yawning and stretching from their night's sleep on the road. Third World . . . you gotta love it!

If you decide to rent a vehicle for transportation, be sure to familiarize yourself with the local driving laws and customs before you do. Even if you do this, know that there are many private rental operators who couldn't care less whether you have proper paperwork or understand the laws. In some countries the mere act of being involved in an accident, regardless of fault, can land you in jail until a hearing is held. Other countries require a foreign driver to buy insurance for the duration of the rental agreement. Failure to do so could cost you jail time or a heavy fine.

Jeff Randall with a rented vehicle along the Nicaraguan border. Not paying attention, ignorance of road conditions, and/or not being able to understand road signs can have detrimental consequences, such as falling into this huge sinkhole in the curve of the road.

Most major rental agencies operating overseas offer supplemental insurance to cover deductible costs and collision damage. Although it's usually an inflated rate, we suggest taking the coverage because standard policies have extremely high deductibles that translate into a lot of out-of-pocket cash if there's an accident. Make sure you understand the contract you're signing, and always keep a copy in your possession because it may be required if misfortune finds you.

Before you venture onto the roads on your own, it's wise to consider the driver mentality in the Third World. Regardless of how careful you are, vehicle operators in other countries may not adhere to the regulations and safety rules you are accustomed to. Driving the speed limit, stopping at stop signs, or yielding to pedestrians may get you run over. The best tools for surviving these situations is studying your destination before departure and taking the time to familiarize yourself with the local customs once in-country.

Even being highly experienced and careful is not an assurance of escaping accidents. During one of our overseas jaunts, we teamed up with renowned adventurer and television host Robert Young Pelton to film a segment for his Travel Channel series, "The World's Most Dangerous Places." Halfway through the project, Pelton rented a small motorcycle for a relaxing tour around a Latin American city. To make a long story short, he was involved in a major accident that landed him in a subpar jungle-town hospital in the care of undertrained doctors. He had to wait more than a week for an emergency flight back to Los Angeles, where he underwent several surgeries to rebuild what the accident and Third World doctors managed to mangle. After surviving the Camel Trophy race (arguably the world's toughest off-road vehicle race), numerous trips into war zones, and a whole host of other unpleasantries, a simple pleasure ride in a Third World city almost cost Pelton his life.

If you must rent a vehicle, then verify that everything is in working order, force the rental agency to record every problem, dent, and scratch, and get a photocopy or carbon copy of this record. Blaming you for preexisting conditions when the vehicle is returned is in an old trick to scam more money from the unwary tourist. During one of our trips to the Panama border, we rented a small Suzuki 4WD vehicle to do a little exploring off the beaten path. After traveling 300 miles down the Pan American Highway we finally hit the backcountry, only to realize the four-wheel drive didn't work. Of course, this was only ascertained after we were in the middle of a flooded low land, axle deep in mud. Luckily, with the help of friendly locals and our climbing gear we were towed to dry land. Our lack of thinking taught us a valuable lesson: Never take the condition of your equipment for granted. Checking and verifying beforehand will save you a lot of problems down the road.

Always carry vehicle emergency kits if you're traveling to remote locations. Extra gasoline, tow rope, jumper cables, potable water, spare tires and belts, duct tape, and miscellaneous hand tools can save the day when it comes to most roadside problems in a strange country. It's also a good idea to bone up on how to handle typical automobile emergencies such as flat tires and overheated engines before you leave home.

Of course there is always the option of hiring a local driver to wheel you around. The advantages to this are obvious. You pay a negotiated rate to get yourself from point A to point B and, just like Greyhound, you leave the driving to them. You don't have to worry about interpreting road signs, getting lost, buying gas, or having an accident that's deemed your fault. The disadvantage is you are at the driver's mercy should he have devious plans or decide he's going to stop by and visit his cousin for four hours (this sort of thing has happened to us on numerous occasions). Another thing to consider is that most local drivers price their services for one way, so after they drop you off at your destination their services are finished. You have to find another driver to bring you back to your starting point, and his rates may not be the same as the first guy's. Depending on your length of stay, it may be possible to hire the driver to layover until you are ready to return. As with everything else in the Third World, ask around and check prices before you settle on a deal.

In underdeveloped countries, rivers are the arteries of life, with homemade boats and rafts the preferred method of transportation. Yet waterway travel can be just as dangerous and scary as traveling on ground because capsizing, crashing, and sinking due to poor boat construction and piloting skills are commonplace occurrences. Life vests, running lights, and safety gear are generally not required or used in remote locations.

If your adventure requires river travel, take a few precautions once you board the craft. In small canoe-type boats, stay seated and balanced in the center of the craft and avoid shifting your weight or standing up. If you're traveling on a large craft, position yourself at the side close to an easy exit, in the back half of the boat rather than the front because most Third World boat drivers pay about as much attention to where they're going as their counterparts on the streets. If you are toward the front and fall off, you are very likely going to be sucked under the boat and killed by the propeller before the driver knows you are gone. Positioning yourself toward the back half of the boat puts you behind the widest part of the craft, thus keeping you from going under should you go overboard.

Before you even get on board, prepare yourself to abandon ship by removing any heavy clothing that can drag you down or hinder swimming. Instead of heavy jackets and warm clothing, use a lightweight poncho to cover yourself if you're cold. Keep all packs unattached to your body anytime you're close to water because they are nothing more than concrete shoes should you fall in and go under. Also remove jewelry or dangling tools that can snag on something and hold you underwater. Even though neck knives are a neat idea, they can become deadly should you become submerged in debris-filled waters.

But what if you are wearing a neck pouch with your cash and important documents? It should be transferred to a waterproof survival kit bag (more on these below) as soon as you board the boat. However, you must discipline yourself to always retrieve the pouch should you leave the boat for any reason.

The authors and their crew ran over a hunter's raft in the middle of the Amazon River with this 30-foot boat, almost costing them their lives at the end of a 16-gauge shotgun.

During our water travels, we always keep some sort of flotation device close by. Empty water bladders or Dry-Seal bags are perfect for this, and they also make great camp pillows or cushions for hard boat seats during extended river travel. In fact, it's a good idea to keep your essential tools and survival kit in a sealed waterproof bag that has not been completely purged of air. The trapped air will help it float, which will prevent your essential gear from sinking to the bottom if you go over the side for whatever reason, and you will have everything with you if you are smart enough to grab the bag before hitting the water. If you have your survival tools in a travel vest or other storage device, place them in the waterproof container once you are on water. Finally, the most important survival tip is to always stay aware and keep a mental note of the closest shoreline in case you have to swim for it.

In 1998 we set out on a three-week expedition to explore the upper reaches of the Amazon River. The trip consisted of traveling more than 300 river miles in a heavy wooden boat propelled by a 50-horsepower outboard motor. Needless to say, when you're hauling 10 people with gear in a 30-foot boat, your rate of travel is relatively slow. Reaching our destination on time required traveling non-stop while sleeping, eating, and performing every other function of life in the boat.

Sometime in the middle of the night, while everyone slept soundly, our craft came to an abrupt, crashing halt. Rushing to the front of the boat, we were met with a shot-gun pointed at our heads wielded by an enraged hunter who was sleeping with his family on a makeshift raft. After several minutes of begging and apologizing in Spanish, we shoved off his river home and continued on our way. The point of this story is that no matter how benign and peaceful it may seem getting to your destination, when you travel in the Third World, nothing is predictable.

CHAPTER 4

Home Away from Home

If you think getting there was a hassle, you haven't seen anything yet.

Once you've reached your destination and laid the basic trip logistics to rest, the remainder of your adventure travel will most likely be done on the fly. Time means nothing in the Third World, and once you immerse yourself in the culture, very few things will go as you planned, so lie back and take things as they happen. Most of all, be willing to change your plans to maintain a degree of safety.

Upon arrival in a foreign country, many travelers check in with the American Embassy (or the embassy of their home country) to get the latest updates and register themselves as being in the country. We suggest learning where the embassy is located and how to get there via several routes should it become necessary. If you choose to visit the embassy in person, try to speak to the Regional Security Officer (RSO). In many countries it is highly unlikely you will get to speak directly with the RSO; instead, you may be handed off to the Consular Services section, which means you may not even end up speaking to an American. Whoever you speak with, ask for a crime fact sheet for the country.

Many travelers, us included, usually forgo a visit to the embassy. We have found that the locals typically have better knowledge of the surrounding areas, and by not visiting we adhere to our rules of maintaining a low profile and staying unattached from any political association. Another reason we avoid embassies is the simple fact that most of their information is old news. Due to the nature of the beast known as the U.S. government bureaucracy, it is perhaps the worst provider of real-time intelligence. By the time information on a real threat has passed through the hands of college-boy analysts and been sanitized for public consumption, it may be too late to help the citizen on the ground. Conversely, the threat potential may have already passed. Even when they do release information, the warnings are usually severely overrated or, worse, underrated.

During our many years of adventure travel, we have requested advice from the U.S. State Department on two separate occasions and, as of this writing, we're still waiting for a response. Our only recourse was to go with our gut feeling on these issues and hope for the best. Just remember that even though government officials want to be in the loop concerning your travels (especially if you are traveling to dangerous places), they are slow to keep you in their loop. Government, by its very nature, hates to lose even the least bit of control. Instead of just telling you straight out that you may be interfering with an operation, they enjoy running all types of games and deceitful strategies, generating paperwork, and increasing payrolls to do nothing but keep an eye on a completely innocent adventurer who has no ill intent. Once you stray into areas normal tourists don't go, they will classify you as crazy, a spy, or someone with criminal intent. The thinking of many government bureaucrats is, "Why would anyone come to a Third World dump for fun?"

If you are traveling to a hostile or remote area and decide to register with the U.S. Embassy, be prepared to hear a dissertation on why you should not do what you are planning. Even though their warnings are sincere in many cases, sometimes their attitude comes from a lack of excitement or purpose in their lives. Being a government employee assigned to an embassy in some shit-hole corner of the world is a boring job, so some of these guys suffer from the I-know-something-you-don't-know syndrome and enjoy playing super spook to occupy their time.

Having said that, the work of embassy employees as a whole should not go unappreciated. They have a job to do, and most of them perform it with honor while providing a valuable service to the United States and its citizens. Of all the U.S. government employees we have drunk beer and swapped war stories with in run-down bars around the world, most of them have been helpful, good folks—true warriors of freedom doing a job most of us would not want to do.

Of course when it comes to government employees, there are always exceptions. One time we were confronted by a self-proclaimed agent for the Centers for Disease Control (CDC), who accused us of being DEA agents because we were visiting "his" tribe of indigenous people that we had previously secured permission to visit. An argument ensued after he demanded we leave. To make a long story short, our team got tired of his mouth and he finally left. After returning to Iquitos, Peru, I learned he had filed several unrelated criminal charges against us. They were later dropped when he could not prove his accusations and the governor of the area backed up our position. We contacted CDC and learned that he had no authority to order travelers out of the area, nor were there any CDC-sanctioned projects in that area. The point is, no matter how nice or innocent you are, egos, jealousy, and control freaks such as this CDC "agent" can cause you problems.

If you are traveling overseas on business or otherwise plan on an extended stay and feel the need for real-time intelligence, consider hiring a private agency that specializes in overseas security. These companies have better resources than the U.S. government when it comes to assisting the civilian traveler. Through a network of indigenous people and trained intelligence professionals, they can provide everything from daily information (e.g., real-time updates on security issues, notice of potential threats based on a network of analysts, and recent information from your home country that may affect your travel plans) to safe houses and evacuation should your situation become desperate. Most of these private firms were established by U.S. government employees retired from agencies such as CIA, Defense Intelligence Agency (DIA), federal law enforcement, and specialized subgroups of the military.

No matter what government public relations brass say about these private operators, they have shown themselves to be far superior to official government channels when it comes to their effectiveness in providing overseas security operations and intelligence. For one, they have less bureaucracy to deal with, which allows them to make decisions quicker. They're also not bound by many of the diplomatic restrictions that hinder the U.S. government. The feds may refuse to take action due to concerns of hurting diplomatic relations, while a private company will be more willing to put the client's safety first instead of worrying about pissing on some diplomat's shoes.

In the end, your security is ultimately your own responsibility, so spend the money for personal attention if you feel your travels may require that level of assistance. When researching private security firms, keep in mind that there are basically two classes of companies. Major players such as Dyncorp, Military Professional Resources Inc., and AirScan typically cater to government and corporate needs, while smaller companies will offer services to individuals and small groups. If your travels consist of conducting business in areas with a high incidence of kidnappings, then research several avenues to protect yourself, including kidnap insurance.

ACQUIRING LOCAL GUIDES

If you haven't prearranged for a local guide, once you are in-country prepare to be greeted by a whole host of indigenous people with extraordinary claims. As already mentioned, Third World "resorts" are typically economies of desperation, with very little regulation of the tourist trade. Just about any local who lives in a metropolitan area and doesn't work a regular job seems to be a tour guide, and the best one in the whole damn country to hear him tell it.

If you are on a typical "eco-tour," your situation is rather easy. Simply asking officials at the airport or checking in with the Department of Tourism will get you hooked up with a registered guide who can show you the usual attractions. However, even going this official route will not guarantee that you will be dealt with honorably. One scam that is common in underdeveloped countries involves officials taking kickbacks from selected guides in return for promoting them to new tourists. We have seen several incidents where this practice ruined the trip for unsuspecting travelers thinking they were getting sound advice. Reputable guides operate mainly by reputation and need no introduction. The two-bit shysters who make their living from an official welfare system usually have no personal motivation, so they end up being poor guides because they are interested only in the dollar, not in doing a good job.

One of our acquaintances who claims to be a professional guide and is on an official's "good guide" list was eventually arrested for operating illegally after taking a group's money, selling the expedition supplies, then cutting the trip short. The tourists were left with nothing to show for their trip of a lifetime. The only consolation they received was witnessing this shyster being taken from the boat in handcuffs.

Be warned that some of these moochers and leeches are expatriate Americans hiding in foreign countries for various reasons, some of which may be criminal. Never fall into the trap of simple comfort. The fact that your new guide is an American and speaks your language should never be reason for letting your guard down. If the country requires guides to have licenses, ask to see his license. If all else fails, visit the local police department and ask them about the guide's reputation.

Similarly, be very wary of any U.S.-based guide service that does not have a track record of providing services. Be sure the one you choose can provide references from past clients and will guarantee what they claim in their advertising. Many of these companies are Web-based and not directly tied to any guide association. Study their Web sites carefully; they are probably not professional guide services if their sites contain generalities and improper spellings of places and people they claim to have access to, and there is a severe lack of knowledge when quizzed about their experiences.

On the other hand, be careful of companies that seem to have an answer for everything or immediately claim they can provide everything you ask for. Remember, true adventure travel is unpredictable. For example if you ask a South American jungle guiding company, "Am I going to see large anacondas in the wilds during my one-week stay?" and they answer with an absolute "Yes!" then they're most likely giving you a sales pitch just to get you to go with them . . . or they plan to take you to a zoo! Use common sense when securing a guide company and question them until you are comfortable they're honest in their dealings and capabilities.

If you decide to acquire a local guide once you're in-country, ask around but never speak in direct terms about your travel objective. Imply that you are merely contemplating what you are there to do. The more excited you seem about going somewhere, the more it will end up costing you. Check with several guides throughout the city, and make a decision based on your gut feeling about the individual.

The number one rule when dealing with a new guide is to always make him quote a price before hiring him. Never offer a price before you hear his offer because he will immediately tell you that it is not enough money even though it may be twice what he typically charges.

When shopping for a guide, always get his contact information instead of giving your contact information to him. A dishonorable guide can use your name and hotel information to his benefit, gaining unauthorized access to your hotel room, for example, simply by telling the receptionist that he's your guide and has been asked to retrieve your bags from the room for a trip departure. Anyone with an honest face and a little bit of personal information about you can pull off a myriad of scams in countries that don't have solid security checks against such things.

Once you choose a guide, never supply a cash deposit or

up-front payment for anything. Some will enthusiastically promise you the world to make the sale and then fall short or lazy once the money is in their pocket. Instead, simply acquire the guide, arrange a meeting place for your trip departure, then be on time for the meeting. Pay as you go, and never pay in full until the services are terminated. Most guides will moan and groan about needing up-front cash to arrange the trip, but don't buy into this unless you have used their services before and established a level of trust. If you feel the guide is requesting a legitimate need for cash to prearrange your trip, go with him and pay for these arrangements personally.

Whatever you do, don't fall into the "feel sorry for me because I'm just a poor guide trying to make an honest living" psychological game some of these folks live by. Even though this may be true, you do not know these people and have to understand that until you do, emotion should never be allowed to interfere with business. Demand and live by mutual respect and honesty when dealing with anyone and you will usually be fine.

Another thing to consider when choosing a guide is that references from the guide's fellow countrymen typically mean nothing. In poorer countries, guiding is a cutthroat business and jealousy is the name of the game. You may have chosen the best guide in the world, but his competitors will always tell you they are better or provide examples of how your guide has screwed other clients. On the flip side, you may have chosen the worst guide in the world and his street hawkers, who are receiving kickbacks, will tell you he can do everything but walk on water.

The best references come from travelers who have used the guide's services in the past. It doesn't take long for a bad guide to become well-known around the world, just as it doesn't take long for the expert guides to establish their reputations. Good guides are those who tell you exactly what can and cannot be done on your planned trip without trying to sugarcoat or exaggerate it to attract your business.

They will also have the experience to give you a firm price and schedule of events without hesitation.

One of the interesting things we see frequently with first-time overseas adventure travelers is a need to take the locals (especially guides) under their wing and support them once the travelers have returned home. If you give out your contact information, such as an e-mail address and phone number, expect letters and phone calls asking for money or "needed" items. Many times the phone calls will be made collect, which can cost a considerable amount.

On one of our past trips, a younger client entered into a deal with a Third World guide against our advice. After returning to the States, he sent the guide more than $2,000 for a harebrained business scheme that never came to fruition. After our client realized he had been shafted, he asked us to help get his money back. We take no responsibility for someone else's stupidity, especially after advising otherwise, so we denied his request, leaving him two grand lighter in the wallet—an expensive lesson in human nature. So know that there is no such thing as an overseas "loan" in the true definition of the word. A loan from an American to a Third World guide is called "free money."

Most guides feel no shame in repeatedly asking for money or other items of value. Many of them see us as rich Americans with more money than we need, never realizing that the cost of living in the United States may in fact be relative to the cost of living in their country. To illustrate our point, we offer this comical but serious e-mail unedited for spelling or grammar. (We did take the liberty of removing names and locations.) It was a response from one of our most trusted guides after we denied his request for another "loan."

SO IF YOU SAY. SO HOW LONG DO YOU THINK IT WOULD TAKE TILL YOU COULD PLACE SOME CASH TO THIS END???. I UNDERSTAND THE SITUATION BUT HERE WE ARE EVEN WORSE. WITH

THE LONG ENDLESS RECESSION. BUT I WILL KEEP PRAYING TILL YOU COME OUT WITH SOMETHING. BUT ANYWAY I WOULD LIKE TO AT LEAST KNOW AN APPROXIMATE TIME. TO TELL MY PEOPLE HERE TO HOLD ON TO THE THING WE HAVE TO DEVELOP HERE.

ANYWAY I THANK YOU FOR YOUR SINCERITY.

DO NOT FORGET TO BRING MORE BAG PACKS AND BANDANAS IN AUGUST. I HOPE THAT WITH THIS WE ARE NOT DISTURBING TO YOU SO MUCH BUT IF WE ARE PLEASE FORGIVE AND I APOLOGIZE. MY SHOES DO NOT FORGET THEY ARE SIZE 8. THE BOOTS FOR THE MILITARY ARE SIZES AS IT FOLLOWS: 7/12 UP TO 9. SHIRTS AND CAMOUFLAGED PANTS ALL SIZES WILL BE FINE. NO WORRIES ON SIZES THAT WILL BE ANY SIZES YOU CAN GET. ALSO DO NOT FORGET THE NIGHT VISION LENS. AND IF YOU CAN ALSO THE GPS. AND I WOULD ALSO LIKE TO KNOW IF YOU COULD GET ME A WIRELESS VIDEO CAMERA ATTACHED TO GPS TO OBSERVE STRATEGICAL PLACES HERE IN (edited) AREA. THAR WIRELESS VIDEO CAMERA IS IT IN THE INTERNET ADVERTISING AND IT IS ON OFFER AT $225.00 USD FOR THE SET OF 3 LENSES THAT CAN BE PLACED IN THE SCHOOL WORK OR SOMEWHERE IN THE STREETS. TO MAKE CHASING OF SOME PEOPLE TO DISCOVER THEIR DAILY ACTIVITIES THAT COULD BE A TRACER. WHATEVER THE PRICE IS I NEED THEM. IF YOU DO NOT BRING THEM ALONG THIS TIME. I WOULD LIKE TO GET

THEM ON THE NEXT TRIP. AND YOU CAN
TAKE IT OUT OF MY FEE ON THE NEXT
TRIP. (JUST THE WIRELESS VIDEO CAM-
ERA.) PLEASE SEND TO ME YOUR REPLY.

It's okay to become friends, and it's even okay to provide gifts and additional cash every once in a while, but
always remember that your adventure's survival and success depends on you always treating your relations with
guides and other service providers as business. Never
promise anything you are not willing to do, and never
allow a guide to nickel-and-dime you to death while he is
providing services. If a guide asks for a loan and you feel
compelled to provide it, do not have any great expectation
of an actual cash return. Instead, acquire some other guarantee of repayment, such as subtracting the loan amount
from the amount you owe the guide at the end of his services, giving the loan in lieu of a normal tip usually paid at
the end of a trip, or giving it in exchange for extra services
not originally agreed on.

CHOOSING GUIDES FOR ABNORMAL TRAVELS

If your destination is a war zone, restricted area, or otherwise taboo locale, a completely different approach may be
required when securing guides. Be very careful of your
methods because merely suggesting travel to these locations
may get you detained or questioned. Never attempt hiring
guides for these areas by mouthing off around town or asking official tourism guides for advice. Finding a competent
guide for dangerous work has no set rules or guidelines; it's
always who you know and how much you trust them to get
you where you need to go. This usually takes a considerable
amount of time and exposure in the country before you can
establish a relationship with someone who is even remote-
ly trustworthy.

Of all the risky things you can do in life, walking into

unfamiliar, hostile territory with a shady guide is comparable to sharing a needle with an AIDS patient. Even if you follow our rules of keeping a good attitude and remaining neutral, the odds of having a successful trip are against you. The upside to this is that guides who will take you into areas where no one else will travel are typically very streetwise and savvy. They usually know every shyster and underworld operator who can bend the law to get you in and out of any dicey situation—for a price, of course. Traveling with these characters has its privileges, but you need nerves of steel and a willingness to accept the negative aspects of their services, since some of their close associates may be drug runners, arms traffickers, smugglers, or any combination of "professions." For the average traveler this is very risky business, and we can't stress enough the importance of avoiding anything that may jeopardize your life or liberty.

Shadowy travel is not only dangerous, it can also be very frustrating. Your main guide will probably not be the person to take you to your final destination, since these types of trips work through a network system. It's nearly always someone who knows someone who knows someone, and you might spend days waiting for approval to advance further. You may be subjected to nonstop questioning and numerous searches, or you may even be blindfolded when traveling. Any hint that you might be a snitch for the opposition may turn your trip into a nightmare. Payoffs and bribes are the norm, and downright failure to complete your goal is usually the outcome.

A few years ago we arranged a trip for a film crew wishing to interview some operators of a jungle cocaine processing laboratory in Central America as well as the U.S. law enforcement operators working against them. This presented a major problem because in such situations trust goes to hell—if the coca processors know you are talking to the government and the government knows you are talking with the narcos, then neither side has any trust in your project or, worse, they try to gain intelligence from you about the opposition. This will occur no matter how neutral you remain.

Acquiring guides for this particular operation proved to be a fiasco. Every time we secured someone and arranged the schedule, something would happen that caused someone to get nervous and the whole thing would start over. One plan was aborted because a guide got spooked over the fact that a member of the media crew had been former military.

Finally, after days of making contacts and waiting around in a run-down hotel, things began to happen. Through several late-night back-alley meetings straight out of a Tom Clancy novel, we were able to get the film team on their way. Once contact was made, the coca processors quickly opened up and placed an amazing amount of trust in the crew. The simple act of the media staff taking no personal position in the debate over drugs—along with a generous offering of cash—bought enough mutual trust to finish the project. At this point we declined any further involvement because we were hired only to make contacts. In this world, you do your job and don't ask questions. The old saying "ignorance is bliss" rings very true because the less you know about some things, the longer you breathe.

We were never successful in getting access to the U.S. government's side of the conflict. As usual, red tape led to problems even after encouraging meetings with on-the-ground operatives. Initially they were receptive to the idea of us accompanying them on an operation, but when the embassy seat shiners got involved, our contacts became cold and that side of the project was scrapped.

This type of adventure travel is best left to those who have done massive amounts of pre-mission research and planning and have established trusted contacts in-country. If you must find a guide for these types of activities, we suggest spending some time in the country away from the tourist areas. Get to know the local populace, and build a reputation for being honest, helpful, and neutral in your

Arranging guides for abnormal travels is dangerous business.
The person who took this photo, Bill Johnson, spent a lot of time
building a good relationship and a level of trust before he was
allowed into this Contra rebel camp. (Bill Johnson photo)

beliefs. Keep your ears and eyes open and slowly associate
yourself with those who appear to be the most helpful for
your goals. Never appear overanxious when the conversation turns to your interests, but always try to keep it as part
of the discussion. After a while change the subject to something different as a way of demonstrating it's not that
important to you. Whatever you do, never blatantly ask for
a guide or information on such hush-hush activities as
going to meet smugglers or rebel leaders.

Good intelligence and trust is built over a period of time.
If you have handled yourself properly, you eventually will
be invited to go along on the trip you are seeking.

Once you secure passage into the dark world, it's very

important that you never become an agent for someone else's cause, be it on the side of government, rebels, unions, religious interests, poor people, or any political faction, no matter how seemingly small or insignificant. Keep your beliefs to yourself and remain neutral to the political attitudes and environment you are traveling in. If MIT graduate and American citizen Lori Berenson had taken this advice, her current address would be in the United States instead of a Peruvian prison. (She made the mistake of befriending and possibly assisting a rebel faction in that country.) If you're traveling as a journalist in the trenches, your job is to report the story, not become part of it. Finally, be simple when it comes to your dress and the items you carry in your clothes. Organization membership cards, certain tattoos, and military type clothing or jewelry can cause you problems.

Some people feel the need to fight oppressive governments over issues of freedom, while others believe their life is to be lived as missionaries for a cause, be it religious or otherwise. If you feel similar compulsions, remember what a wise man once said: Wearing your heart on your sleeve only offers a good target. Regardless of your honorable intentions, you may find yourself injured, imprisoned, kidnapped, or killed should something go wrong. So if your head is set on fighting for a cause and you believe your contribution will help save the world, be prepared to accept the consequences of your work. Whether you're on a mission for religion, freedom, or a free press, there will always be folks who don't trust your motives and guides whose loyalty is auctioned to the highest bidder. Missionaries, mercenaries, and journalists are typically an expendable commodity in the Third World because their goals are focused and they lose the survival premise of remaining impartial.

As Bill Johnson found out with the Afghan/Soviet war, it is difficult to just interject yourself in the midst of dangerous places regardless of your good intentions. But it is not impossible. After his experience in Afghanistan, he traveled to Nicaragua with $1,000 and a Spanish dictionary in his pocket. After being rejected by Nicaraguan Contra leaders and thrown out of their camps on more than one occasion, he was finally allowed to work as a volunteer battlefield medic. Having paid his dues the hard way, he realized that persistence, patience, and keeping your trust network small and private are the keys to success—not to mention a little bit of luck.

Whatever you do and wherever you go, always remember that some day you may want to come home to the United States. One of the best rules to follow, therefore, is to never do anything against U.S. foreign policy or break U.S. law. Enlisting in or aiding a foreign military can get your citizenship revoked, saddle you with criminal charges for a Neutrality Act violation, and even sacrifice certain protections you may have under international treaties. Back in the 1980s an acquaintance of ours, Tom Posey, was charged with violation of the Neutrality Act simply for supplying clothing and food to the Nicaraguan Contras through the Civilian Military Assistance (CMA) organization. Of course it was okay that the U.S. government was funneling arms to the Contras, but when a private organization decided to help out, the feds didn't like it. Go figure.

Adventuring to the other side of the tracks can be fun, educational, and invigorating in the short term, but in the long haul the odds are stacked against you in more ways than you know. If you must wear your beliefs on your sleeve and fight for a cause, prepare yourself to deal with folks on all sides who will do whatever it takes to fulfill their ultimate goal of power and dollars. The loss of your life means absolutely nothing to anyone but your family, so make sure your life insurance is paid up.

SELECTING A HOTEL

If you don't mind living simply, one of the greatest bargains of Third World travel can be found in the hotels. For only a few dollars a day you can stay in a private room or spend less and live in a community hostel. Unless you're traveling with a group, we recommend securing private accommodations since hostels have a reputation for petty theft and problems from other travelers.

When you check in you will usually be asked to provide your passport for registration. Along with the standard information, you may be asked to write down your current occupation. If you are military, police, or any other profession that may raise suspicions, then lie and give a nonthreatening occupation such as school teacher. In countries of turmoil or where the power structure may change quickly, it's best to be known as a nonthreat. Should a rebel faction take control of your area or a full-blown coup d'état take place, there may be people searching hotel records to find out who is in their town and how much of a threat they pose. Even worse, certain factions will directly search out any American that represents authority for the purpose of kidnapping or killing to make a public statement.

Throughout our travels, we have found that small, run-down hotels on the outskirts of town usually provide more security and a pleasant atmosphere. Avoiding the downtown areas keeps you away from the noise, crowds, and other tourists (the biggest problems we've faced in foreign hotels always came from other travelers and not the local populace). Staying out of town also gives you an advantage if the political atmosphere changes overnight. The inner city will be the first area locked down, giving you advance warning and time to institute your bug-out plan.

Many security experts will advise you to keep your passport locked inside a hotel safe and a copy of the passport on your person while you're out on the town. In some countries, such as Belarus, it is required to leave your passport with your official hotel of residence, and you will be charged a fee for this service. If your travels take you to a country where this is not required, then our advice is exactly opposite of what the security professionals suggest. If given the option, never trust anyone, including hotels, with your travel documents.

Common sense dictates that should you be away from your hotel and all hell breaks loose, why have the added worry of getting back to your hotel to retrieve your valuables? So keep a copy of your passport at the hotel or other secure location, an extra copy with a friend or family member in your home country, and your original securely on you at all times. If you're mugged or robbed of the original, then use the copies to obtain another. Street crime or losing a passport is an isolated event that no longer poses a threat after it's over. On the other hand, major political upheaval is not isolated, and not having your passport during these times can have serious consequences, especially since embassy officials may be too busy to offer help to the average traveler. Time is critical if unexpected, dangerous events happen, and those who are able to move immediately without side trips to retrieve valuables will have the best chance of escaping.

When you arrive at your hotel, the first thing you want to look at is its overall security. Is the main entrance locked after hours? Does your room have windows allowing you to exit via an alternate route during an emergency? Do the doors have the ability to be securely locked? Many remote area hotels may not have very secure settings, but as a general rule, it is still better to stay out of town than to move into town for an extra-secure hotel.

With multilevel hotels, it's still hotly debated among security experts as to which floor is the safest. Naturally the bottom floor is best for escaping fires, while higher floors may be better in possible earthquake areas, but our focus in this book is safety from the human element. We prefer to stay on a second floor because the bottom floors are usually the first to be occupied or crowded when chaos takes over. A second-floor room with a window allows you to escape if need be and also gives you an additional few minutes of time should dangerous events on the street spill into the hotel.

Once inside your hotel room, keep the doors locked and

place a chair or heavy object in front of the door for added security. Keep your important valuables packed so they can be picked up in a hurry during an evacuation. Be tidy and keep everything organized. There's nothing worse security-wise than to have all your gear strewn across the room and have to search to find something when you need it.

Leave a light on when you go out for daily activities, and if your room has a television, leave it on also. When you are off the premises, do not leave your room key with the receptionist. If you keep it with you, then you are in control of the access to your room should you need to retreat there in a hurry or run back to get something due to sudden changes in a country's political climate. Self-sufficiency, no matter how small in scope, adds to your overall survival potential.

Some people use thin travel cable locks to secure nonessential luggage when they are out of their rooms. Although this may help prevent petty pilfering, it also attracts the attention of those who may be looking for your valuables. This is a personal call for the traveler.

When sleeping at night, keep your clothes arranged for quick response. We leave our wallets, keys, and papers inside our clothes alongside a fully packed survival vest. Should something happen in the middle of the night, we can be dressed and out of the hotel in less than three minutes with everything needed to make it to safety.

Finally, the most important rule about living in a hotel is taking the time to know where you are and having several routes of escape. Keep a mental map in your head of how to get to safe zones, be it the embassy, a friend's residence, or other predetermined safe house. Research your area at night as well as in the daytime because street lighting, busy streets, and other factors will change according to the time of day.

RESTAURANTS

Restaurants can range from classy high-end establishments to open-air cafes with fuel oil poured on the dirt floor to keep dust and flies down. Small restaurants usually have a very limited menu, maybe only the one entree they are making that particular day.

When it comes to the food itself, *lean* is the word outside the United States, and in the Third World it is very lean. Chicken and beef will be very lean and consequently somewhat tough. Fish is usually excellent. Everything is served with rice, the staple food of the Third World. The serving sizes are usually very large, so you do get your money's worth.

If the area's water quality is questionable, order bottled water, soda with no ice, or beer. If you do not specify water "without gas," you will probably get bottled carbonated water, which is common throughout Latin America. The designer stuff labeled as "pure spring water" in the States is not as hot a commodity in the Third World.

We prefer to frequent local restaurants over American-owned fast-food chains. Just about every major city in the world has a McDonald's, and it always seems to attract the most tourists. If we're adventuring overseas, the last place we want to eat is where all the other Americans are gathered, not to mention the fact that we can usually eat a full meal cheaper in a local restaurant than what we would pay for a Quarter Pounder in the same city.

There is another good reason to eat in local establishments. If anti-American sentiment is running high, any American-owned franchise seems to have a lot of spite taken out on it during bursts of anarchy. Many dumb-ass rioters will burn down buildings they believe are representative of America.

Finally, even if there are good relations between the host country and the United States, most panhandlers and moochers have learned to hang out around well-known fast-food joints because that's where all the rich Americans go when they visit their country.

COMMUNICATIONS

Depending on the country and area you're visiting, communications can range from the latest in high-speed Internet and digital telephony to no access at all. We continue to be amazed how some of the poorest countries in the world seem to spare no expense updating their communications infrastructure. Internet cafés, cellular phones, and high-speed electronic switching are commonplace in larger cities worldwide these days.

Before you leave home, contact your long-distance provider to get a local access number for the country you are visiting. This will be needed to reach an operator who speaks your language and use your calling card number to make a long-distance call. If you decide to use the convenience store phone cards, make sure they are capable of calling from the country you are visiting. Even though these cards are probably the most secure way to make long-distance calls, we don't care to travel with them because they have preset time allotments. If you get in a real jam, you may need a lot more time than the cards allow. Whatever card you choose for communication, just be sure to practice common-sense security methods by making sure no one can see the credit card or PIN number you dial.

As a backup plan, always have a contact person in the United States who will accept a collect call. If you just need to check in and let everyone know you're fine without it costing anyone, then decide on a false name and give it to your contact person before you leave. Explain to them that once you arrive at certain destinations, you will make a collect call under this false name. When the operator asks if they will accept the call, all they need to do is decline and this will inform them you have arrived at your location safely. If you need them to accept the call, then make it under your real name. With this system, you can come up with several names coded for different locations or statements you need to convey. Just make sure that you leave a copy of the code sheet with the contact person.

If you plan to stay in touch via the Internet, set up a Web-based e-mail account (such as hotmail) before you depart. Many Internet cafés do not allow access to private e-mail POP accounts or mail servers, so your best bet is to have an account you can access through a Web browser from anywhere. Many of the larger Internet access providers already offer Web-based mail that allows you to check your private account from anywhere in the world, but this needs to be set up and tested before you depart.

When using e-mail as your primary communication, try to keep messages short and to the point. Write notes of what you need to e-mail before logging on since this will keep your time online to a minimum and the cost down.

When using any type of communication from a foreign country, never take privacy for granted. Keep your messages sanitized, and don't elaborate on anything that could cause you trouble.

If you must report sensitive information via e-mail, then set up a mail drop account. This is a Web-based e-mail account for which you and a chosen contact both know the login and password. It is only used as a central gathering location for information. In other words, users never send e-mail from the drop box account and only log on to check for new information received from other e-mail accounts. When sending e-mails to this account, do so through one of the numerous Web-based e-mail sanitizing sites such as anonymizer.com.

A drop account works like this. An e-mail is sent to the account through a sanitizer that removes all originating information from the e-mail. The user it is intended for logs on to the account and reads the e-mail. After reading it, the user moves the information from the in box to the sent box. If the original sender wants to make sure the e-mail has been read, he simply logs on to the drop account and makes sure the e-mail has been moved to the sent box. Although this system is not foolproof, it does add a layer of additional security for travelers in hostile areas who need to communicate with a trusted contact some-where else in the world.

CHAPTER 5

City Life

Compared to all the remote villages, hard bush, and adverse wilderness we have traveled through around the world, none of it has had the same potential for danger as major cities. Sure, the bush has wild animals, venomous creatures, and dirty conditions with the potential for causing harm, but the greatest risk to man has always been other men.

Unlike the animal world, humans are born with a trusting nature, even in the face of imminent danger. Somehow we just can't believe there are people in the world who place no value on life or would actually harm us for a few dollars worth of material possessions. Surprisingly, once someone leaves the comforts of home and takes up traveling in a foreign land, this trusting nature seems to manifest itself even more. This is typically caused by feeling out of place and having a natural need to communicate in order to bring about a sense of reality in the new surroundings. Many times these abnormal feelings will cause a traveler to trust folks they would otherwise be skeptical of. Yet for every trusting traveler, there are at least ten con artists or criminals ready to take advantage of their human nature. These exploits can range from simple beggars in the street to large-scale criminal acts against tourists.

Large cities in any country have always been a haven for moochers, looters, thugs, and various other criminal types. The reason for this is simple: Cities offer the criminal entrepreneur a larger target market due to population and tourism. Plus, the criminal has a whole host of survival tools available to him that don't require much work to attain, including shelter, transportation, food and water, and in most cases free medical services. If he finally gets caught mugging a tourist, the prison system is typically so overcrowded that he will be back on the streets very quickly.

In contrast, small Third World communities and remote villages are usually far removed from government services and support. Survival is a common effort among the locals, and there is little tolerance for the average criminal or lazy bum. Many times those caught in criminal acts are dealt with swiftly by the local residents, and the police or government authorities never know about the case. We have learned about several cases in which people caught committing crimes in remote villages were never heard from again. In one such incident, a small Mexican village rendered its own justice without consulting the authorities after a resident there killed his friend in a drunken argument—they buried him alive alongside the body of his dead friend.

Besides the common street thug, large cities have many other dangers associated with them. When politically based riots break out, they generally occur in capital cities and larger economic districts. I once traveled to Jakarta, Indonesia, on a business trip in the late 1990s. Shortly after arriving, the famed Jakarta riots broke out. Although I was safe in my hotel, the streets had dissolved into a war zone of hurtling rocks, tear gas, and rubber and real bullets.

I would be lying to you if I said it wasn't an adrenaline rush to be in the middle of it all, but even though I was safe, the peripheral implications eventually took their toll. When uprisings like this happen, the already weak infrastructures of these countries break down, and services begin to degrade even for the noncombatants. In my case, when it was time for me to leave, I found all the airline phones jammed, and many carriers were canceling flights. All the foreign embassies were packed, and services were down to a crawl. I was finally able to rebook a flight with the help of a local friend and get back to the United States.

Trust me: In these situations, no one gives a damn about you. The only ways to make yourself safe are to use good judgment, have an ability to buy your way out of the mess, or bug-out to smaller, less-affected towns and villages.

Another thing to consider about cities is that larger populations always generate more filth and disease. Third World cities usually lack the services to support the population, resulting in utilities shortcutting on quality to keep up with demand. Due to this "quantity before quality" necessity, the water, transportation, and sewage systems are sorely lacking compared to progressive countries.

Consequently, never be deceived by luxurious trappings in the Third World. Although they may have the appearance of luxury, the system that feeds the low-rent district is probably the same system feeding these establishments. As an example of this, we frequent a beautiful hotel in the middle of a rustic turn-of-the-century frontier-type city in South America. For $90 a night, you get polished marble floors, air conditioning, a luxurious elevator ride to your room, indoor heated pool, and every other amenity imaginable. Having stayed there several times, one day I decided to check out the "nerve center" of this place. To my surprise, the hotel's sewage was dumping into the river just as it did from every other building in the town, and water to the hotel was supplied by an open cistern from the river.

Generally speaking, large cities are for folks who want the nickel tour—in other words, the glossy brochure traveler. Remote places give the adventurer face-to-face reality without the appearance of safety and comfort. In these areas, a traveler is less likely to take his personal safety for granted. For example, when the traveler sees that his drinking water comes directly from the river, he will be sure to purify it instead of assuming it's safe as he does when it's taken from a brass faucet in a fine hotel.

Simply put, the outward appearance of highly populated tourist areas is designed to attract as much money as possible. In order to do this, these regions must maintain a facade of comfort and safety, and for the most part they are successful. However, the bowels of the system can pose a very serious threat to the unsuspecting traveler.

LOCAL POLICE AND MILITARY

Hollywood movies have created an enormous amount of fear for first-time travelers to the Third World. For instance, one of the questions we always get asked by new

Although major foreign cities can be beautiful, never allow the allure to dampen your common sense. Beauty is often only skin deep in most tourist areas.

adventurers is how many cops we've had to pay off to get ourselves out of jams. We typically refuse to answer this because the few times we have given a "gift" of money, it was usually done to expedite some unusual request that we needed done rather than to get our asses out of a tight spot, a distinction a new traveler may not understand.

Sadly, many people believe that Third World government officials survive only by feeding off unsuspecting tourists, either by framing them with drugs or accusing them of crimes. Although this phenomenon certainly does exist, it is not common for most travelers and tourists to run up against it. In fact, every "legitimate" story along these lines that we have researched has panned out to be one of two things: 1) the person arrested was doing something illegal, or 2) it was a pure urban legend told by someone who knew someone who had a cousin that was arrested in Mexico. The story will always go something like this: "And this man was doing nothing illegal. They just singled him out and arrested him. Then they offered to let him go if he could pay X amount of dollars."

Police and military units in foreign countries have always treated us with respect and been more than fair in every dealing we've had with them. In fact, a lot of American cops could learn a lot about manners and respect from their foreign counterparts. What's so funny is that American movie makers have always portrayed foreign "secret police" and military officers as being cold and calculating assholes, while our own law-enforcement officers are depicted as courteous and respectful, paying full attention to due process and constitutional rights. Well, people busted on American soil may enjoy more rights *after* the arrest, but I can assure you that the respect given to a citizen in many Third World countries before the arrest is far greater than what is afforded by some of the adrenaline-junkie cops we have patrolling our own streets these days.

On several occasions we have been party to interactions between foreign law enforcement and private citizens (both American and foreign nationals). One such incident occurred on one of our first trips overseas. A local guide of ours—who it turned out had purchased some articles on credit and not paid for them—accompanied me to the bank to change some money. As soon as we walked into the bank, we were surrounded by red berets and uniforms. The police explained they had a warrant for this individual's arrest and would be taking him to the police station. I explained that I was simply there to change some money and needed the guide to translate for me. The police then told the guide to take care of the translation for me and meet them outside.

After we finished our business, the guide walked outside and went to the police station. No handcuffs and no sarcastic attitude. I arrived at the police station soon after that and was treated like a VIP. The police chief introduced himself, brought me a cup of coffee, apologized for having to arrest our guide, and then explained what we needed to do to clear the matter up. We made arrangements with the accuser to pay the debts, and everyone walked out of the police station and proceeded with our adventure plans. This ordeal made a deep impression on me.

Since this incident there have been numerous times when we were involved in similar matters, and each time they were handled with professionalism and courtesy. I believe that our good fortune has been a direct result of our being honest and respectful and keeping our egos in check. On the other hand, another acquaintance of ours was on an expedition in South America that involved traveling into an area known for drug smugglers. On the return trip down river, his boat was stopped and searched by narcotics police. This acquaintance, not knowing much Spanish, attempted to impress the officers with his fake Special Forces ring and tattoos, actually causing more suspicion and time delays than he would have by simply keeping his mouth shut.

Some basic rules to live by when approached by foreign military or police officers are to be courteous and do as you are asked. Remember, in another country you do not have a lot of the rights you have in the United States, so if an officer wants to search your car or bags, allow him to do so without causing a major scene or getting upset. Answer any questions truthfully, but don't volunteer information or try to impress anyone with your knowledge or how much of a badass you think you are. If you do not understand what is being asked, make that known to them by giving a nonthreatening body gesture or saying "I don't understand" in English. *Never* answer a yes or no question that you don't understand. If for some reason you are detained or taken somewhere, do your best to let someone know what is happening and where you are going.

If you are put in jail, the first call you are allowed to make should be to the American Embassy or your own country's embassy if you're not a U.S. citizen. (Even though we typically avoid embassies, this is a situation in which they will initially be most helpful.) The embassy officials will ask a series of questions to establish your identity and the reason why you are there and to formulate a plan of action to assist you. Allow them the time to get this information from you without interrupting. Answer the questions and provide additional information that you feel may be beneficial to your release. Do not speculate, get upset, or provide any false information, and never threaten any foreign or American government official.

As a general rule, we have found foreign police and military in some countries to be very trusting of American tourists, especially the officers who man remote outposts. During a visit to Nauta, Peru, I decided to drop in on the National Police to introduce myself. As I arrived, two young officers were walking in soaking wet from a riverene operation. I told them I was visiting their town and jungle regions and wanted to see what the police station looked like. They invited me into their office, where we talked for a few minutes. Soon we were discussing weapons, and one of the officers handed over his AK with full magazine for me to inspect. I was amazed because I knew no American cop would ever hand a loaded weapon to a foreign stranger. Out of courtesy, I gave a close inspection and a nod of approval to his AK, then handed it back. He immediately drew his Taurus .38 revolver and handed it to me. Again, I pulled my inspection and gave a gesture of approval before returning it. I didn't have the heart to tell him his service revolver was on its last legs and almost too loose to shoot safely. I spent several hours at the station learning a lot about what they did and how they conducted many of their

Police and military officials in remote locations are typically more laid-back than their city counterparts. These officers from a small country in Central America allowed us to target shoot with their M16s and ride patrol with them while searching for a few wanted bandits.

remote antinarcotic operations. Just before leaving I had them lock me in their jail and had a friend take a photo.

Manners and respect aside, in some ways the police and military of foreign countries are not that much different from our own. The larger the city, the less "Mayberry" friendly the officers will usually be, and the more channels you will have to go through to get something done. Fortunately, we have always managed to receive professional attention and access to the things we needed to make our expeditions successful. During our travels in South

America, we have participated in military training and operations on numerous occasions, had dinner with top military officials, toured military bases, lived in military barracks, received military/police support and equipment for our expeditions into dangerous areas, and been stumbling drunk with many police chiefs and their officers in all-night party sessions. We have been able to do this because of trust—trust that extends not only from those officials to us, but from us to those officials.

The bottom line when dealing with any government personnel is to be honest and friendly, keep a smile on your face, never try to convince them you're something that you're not, and, most importantly, leave your politics at home and present yourself as a neutral person in search of nothing but knowledge and enjoyment.

PERSONAL SECURITY

While traveling through large foreign cities, personal security is quite simply the individual traveler's responsibility. Somewhere along the line (but especially after the events of September 11, 2001), many people have come to the conclusion that their personal safety is the responsibility of public officials or government agencies such as the military and police. Nothing could be further from the truth. These organizations cannot assure anyone of absolute safety, and all too often they are the guys who mop up the scene long after someone has been victimized. In order to travel safely, you must expect the unexpected, be confident in your ability to handle quick-changing environments, and have the tools, skills, and mental capacity to act decisively if the situation dictates that you must.

Over the years we have had many new travelers explain their trip agenda and then ask, "Is it legal for me to carry a firearm there for personal defense?" Our response has always been, "Why would you want to do that?" They usually reply with a hundred stories they had heard about the dangers of traveling abroad and feel they need some means of protection.

First of all, let's get something straight here: To do adventure travel means accepting a certain amount of risk. If you're too scared to face a country's populace without a firearm, then join the military (no disrespect meant to the military) or stay at home, because if you don't feel capable without the security blanket of a gun, you're going to make a piss-poor adventure traveler. Even if you had a firearm and were in a situation that required its use, you'd probably already be outgunned. A Colt .45 is not going to be much security against rebel forces armed with submachine guns, squad automatic weapons, and hand grenades. Simply maintaining a neutral attitude has a much better chance of keeping you alive if you're ever confronted by a hostile force. Once again, in your travels always give the impression of being unimportant. A gun will almost always make you appear to be a threat.

Oh, so you think you need a firearm for the common street thug, huh? Well, go ahead and cap a criminal in a Third World country and see how long it takes you to get out of prison. The only thing a gun is going to do in a foreign country is make you a target and/or combatant. The only time we would suggest picking up a gun is as a last-ditch effort to save your ass. If the government has folded and the country has gone to shit, there's anarchy in the streets, and warlords have directed the mobs to kill foreigners on sight, then by all means find, steal, or kill for whatever weapon you can get your hands on and use it to get yourself across the border or to a safe zone. It is highly unlikely this scenario will ever present itself, though.

There is no magic bullet to keep the individual traveler safe at all times. Situations change, and what you prepare or practice for may be totally different than any actual incident that may take place. Forget about physical self-defense techniques as your first line of defense—common sense, awareness, and self-confidence are by far the security tools of choice. Proper attitude and appearance will keep you alive much longer in foreign countries than being heavily armed or trained in the latest ninjutsu techniques.

Once you're moving about the landscape, don't be an obvious American. Many indigenous people may not particularly like your country, so why push it? In areas where anti-American sentiment is particularly high, some travelers have chosen to identify themselves as Canadian to avoid trouble. This is fine if you are dealing with locals on the street; if you are dealing with government officials, it is best to tell the truth. Whatever you do, keep a firm smile on your face and be pleasant to those you meet. At the same time, make yourself a hard target by having the attitude that you refuse to be an easy victim. Show confidence without being aggressive. Avoid dealing with panhandlers by simply saying "no." Refuse to enter into an argument by politely walking away.

Of all the crimes committed against Americans in foreign countries, petty theft is at the top of the list. Much of this can be blamed on the way we dress and conduct ourselves. Robert Pelton described many of the American tourists as "obvious as a naked man with $100 bills taped to his body." Expensive jewelry and clothing can easily turn you into a victim. Although it may be impossible to do so completely, try to blend with the local populace as much as possible. Only carry small baggage when walking around tourist areas. The more stuff you're carrying, the bigger and easier target you become. You want to stay light and loose just in case you have to make a quick dash to avoid being hit by a crazed taxi driver or otherwise run for your safety.

As discussed earlier, when it comes to your spending cash, we suggest having a throwaway wallet *and* keeping loose bills wadded up in your pocket. The remainder of your money is kept out of public eye at all times. The reason for this is because every Third Worlder knows that Americans carry wallets, so simply using the pocket cash may not keep them from robbing you of the wallet they know is there. If you're robbed, give them the few loose bills and the throwaway wallet that they *will* demand.

If you're carrying camera or video equipment, use a secure travel vest to store your film, batteries, and extra gear while moving throughout the city. This keeps the whole system neat and on your person at all times and makes it much easier to hop buses and other local transportation.

In many countries American military personnel are not welcome, so trying to impress the police or native populace with your Special Forces rings, jewelry, or tattoos is an excellent way to be targeted for trouble. Dressing in a military style is even worse. Some indigenous people view foreign military personnel as bullies and threats and will go out of their way to show the gringo Rambo they can kick his ass. It's a pride thing, and it only causes problems.

If you're a businessman working overseas, avoid traveling in vehicles with your business name on them, and be careful of advertising yourself with business cards or company logo gear in public. Again, dress down and look unimportant and you will be better off.

Once you're in the city, always take a day to relax and settle in before jumping headlong into your tour or adventure. Pick up a local English-language newspaper and see what the climate is like. The locals and the press will usually warn you of coming problems quicker than the embassies and other officials. Listen to the rumors and always trust your gut feeling.

Although all of our team members feel confident roaming solo in the larger cities that we frequent, the best security is to always travel with one or more companions. Not only does it make you a harder target for isolated theft and petty crime, but it also keeps official focus off you. A single out-of-place person roaming through a nontourist section of the city will be seen as suspicious in a lot of countries, but a group of tourists wandering through that same area will not.

Awareness and trusting your gut feeling will help you avoid most problems, but only if you listen to what your senses are telling you. A few seconds of advanced warning may mean the difference between life and death. In every bad situation I have been in, be it a fight or otherwise, there was a sense of "oh shit" that came across me just before the lightning struck. Many times this has saved my ass by prompting me to quickly make a safe exit before the chaos hit. The problem with most individuals is that they are too preoccupied to listen to what their bodies are telling them. Awareness gives you the ability to avoid an incident altogether or at least an advance warning to enable you to counter a situation that's unavoidable.

Avoid any situation that makes you nervous, and never be too proud to run. When in doubt, just get away as fast as you can. There's no shame in avoiding a fight and living to tell about it. If you can't get away, be prepared to use every dirty trick in the book to protect yourself. Forget about all of those roundhouse kicks, ridge hands, and other martial arts tactics that take years of repetition to be effective in a real fight. Resorting to natural reflexes such as kicking, punching, pinching, biting, or hitting your attacker with a rock will go a lot further in your defense.

Just before you make your move, always divert your opponent's attention. If nothing else, start singing the theme song to *The Sound of Music* at the top of your lungs—anything to create a surprise or momentary distraction to implement your plan of running, hitting the guy with a brick, kicking him in the nuts, head butting his nose, or slamming him in the throat. Whatever you end up doing, do it with every ounce of power in your body. Never attempt to wound or pull punches; there is no such thing as dirty fighting when your life is on the line. Divert attention, then make an overwhelming move without hesitation. The secret to winning a real fight is to make the fight uglier to your opponent than it is to you. And always remember: as soon as you get an opening, run like hell.

Never enter into a physical fight with a common crook over money, a car, your camera, or any other material thing. If you're outgunned, use the valuables to open an escape route by throwing them on the ground, getting out of the car, or any other move that allows the perp to achieve his goal, then get the hell out of Dodge. Many times, continuing to talk and move while looking for an escape route or safe zone will get you out of a situation without physical harm.

Finally, never allow yourself to be taken from the scene of the initial confrontation by force. If the criminal decides he is going to force you into a car or escort you to another place, make your stand there and make it quickly. The odds are against you living another day if you leave the scene. If you cannot run, fight with everything you have, even if you're being held at gunpoint. It's better to be shot on a public street than killed in a secret location. At least you have a chance of getting medical care, and once the shot is taken, the criminal will most likely flee the area quickly.

Kidnap victims in the Third World don't have much chance of being found alive unless they have a ton of ransom money available to them. To avoid being the victim of a kidnapping, it is important that you never settle into a daily routine. Most kidnap victims are studied carefully before being taken hostage. If you have to stay in a city for an extended period, be sure to alternate the way you drive to work, the times you come and go to your hotel, and any other routine that makes you predictable and therefore vulnerable.

THREAT RESPONSE PLANNING

Any time you travel into potentially hostile territory, you should always have an emergency response plan should things turn sour. If you're in a remote area of the country, you will probably be less affected than if you are in a larger city. The downside to remote areas is they have little access to international travel facilities, so leaving quickly by the normal routes may be out of the question.

It has been said that underdeveloped countries are

always ripe for revolution. Just like a dormant volcano, it's not whether it's going to explode but when. If you pay attention to world affairs, you know that political turmoil or some revolutionary group can rear its head in just about every Third World region. Most of the time it's nothing more than an occasional car bombing, but sometimes it can be more widespread and severe, with governments changing overnight and anarchy reigning in the streets the next morning.

Usually the mood on the street will warn the traveler that something's not right, sort of like the calm before the storm. It may manifest itself by increased military or police activity throughout the city, more frequent press briefings by government figureheads, larger than normal political rallies, increased security around government buildings and airports, and numerous other things that make you realize that something is going on and you're not getting the full story. This is another example of one of those nagging gut feelings that should be trusted.

Once this atmosphere begins to develop, you should be on your way to the airport or border. If you wait too long, the lines will be jammed and you will more than likely be stuck (as happened to me in Jakarta, Indonesia). When the shit really hits the fan, be prepared to pay highway robbery rates to taxi drivers and for every other service. If the city is in total anarchy, don't argue about price as long as it gets you to safety and you have the cash to pay. Travel light and leave your main baggage behind. Take anything that will be of importance to your survival and leave the souvenirs, spare clothes, and fancy luggage for the looters. Some folks may argue that these could be useful barter or bribe goods, but it's not worth the added time to take that chance. If anything, offer it to your taxi driver in exchange for passage out of the city.

If you happen to be on foot and come upon looters, rioters, or any crowd of bad folks, try to avoid eye contact and keep moving away from the action. Don't run unless it's

Increased military and police presence, along with large gatherings of protestors, should be your first sign of coming trouble in Third World cities.

necessary. Running brings out the animal instinct in predators and could cause them to direct their attention to you. Walk away briskly, remaining on full alert as to what's going on behind you as you keep scanning up ahead, looking for safe areas to hide in or escape to should it become necessary.

The last resort if you're in the midst of an angry mob with no obvious means of escape is to join them. You might just pull it off if you can convince the crowd that you're there to wreak havoc, loot color TV sets, and throw rocks at the cops too. Always remember that in just about any state of anarchy, in the beginning the mobs are the ruling force. It usually takes time for the police and military to implement a plan of action and become a viable threat to the crowds. Go with the winning side until you can escape. Screw principles, beliefs, and laws if stubbornly adhering to them may cost you your life.

If you make it through the rock throwers, you have several options. You can go to the airport and try to get a flight out, head overland to an alternate border crossing, go to the U.S. Embassy and hope you get in, leave the city for a more remote location, or sit tight and ride it out.

If the situation has progressed to total anarchy, you're most likely not going to catch a flight out because everyone who's not a citizen will be at the airport trying to do the same thing. Heading overland to a border would depend on the neighboring country and its proximity to where you are. The U.S. Embassy may be a possibility, but you know where the mobs will converge if the radical factions are pissed off at the United States. Leaving the city for a more remote location may buy you some time to develop a plan of action away from the chaos, but then there's always the possibility of running into other badasses in the boonies, especially with countries in revolution. Sitting tight is an option if you know a local whom you can trust to keep you in a safe house. The bottom line is there is no definite answer in a situation such as this because it depends on the circumstances. Keeping your options open, assessing the threat (Is it simple mob chaos, revolution, a government coup, or foreign attack?), refusing to panic, and not always following the masses are your best survival techniques once you're in the middle of it.

Your pre-trip research will have provided the answers to a lot of the above questions, and once you know the danger potential you can better formulate your bug-out plan should something go wrong. Whatever you do, continue to be aware while you're in a foreign city. Take its pulse daily, and if you sense something's wrong, make your move before it boils over. Waiting on the State Department to issue a travel advisory or warning may be too late.

Familiarize yourself with the city, and learn several routes that lead to safe areas, be it the embassy, airport, remote village, or neighboring country. Keep a map of the country as well as a city map on your person at all times, and be sure you study and understand them.

Finally, pack a few worst-case survival tools in your travel survival bag discussed in Chapter 2. These items should include a Bic lighter, pack of cigarettes (even if you don't smoke), extra cash, credit card, phone card, first-aid kit, small flashlight with spare batteries, pencil and paper, a multitool (Leatherman, Gerber, etc.) or multiple-use pocket knife, and a small compass just in case you need to orient yourself or have to travel on foot. The bladed items can be added after you land at your destination, because you won't be able to have them in your bag when you fly.

EMERGENCY HEALTH ISSUES

Next to threats to your personal security, having an accident or medical problem that requires hospitalization is the biggest concern of adventure travel. Imagine this scenario: You arrive at your final destination in some remote, run-down part of the world. As you make your way down the steps of the plane, you fall and break your leg. The next thing you know, some nasty little man, jabbering in an unknown tongue, is loading you into a makeshift ambulance. Once you arrive at the hospital, you notice the place looks more like where you take your deer to be dressed during hunting season than a medical facility. Sound outlandish? Believe me, it's not.

First things first. Before you take off for your adventure into never-never land, check with your health insurance provider to see if you are covered while overseas. If not, then ask about purchasing a separate insurance rider for the period of time you plan on being abroad. You may also want to check with the numerous companies that offer emergency medical evacuation insurance. Basically what this does is get you out of the local slaughterhouse and return you home to be worked on by your own doctors. Also be sure to notify your personal doctor of how long you will be gone and where you are traveling to, and have your doctor's emergency contact information packed with you.

Even with all of this in place, emergency medical care may still have to be performed in the host country. If this happens and you're still conscious, do your best to secure a good translator so you can communicate accurately with the medical personnel taking care of you. It's also wise to include a medical history sheet inside your passport so primary care facilities will be able to determine vital information about you should you be unable to talk or communicate. If you have a life-threatening allergy to some medication such as penicillin, it's not a bad idea to write this out in both English and the regional language.

If it is a serious accident, make a call to your personal doctor as soon as you arrive at the hospital. If you are unable to communicate, it should be prearranged with your traveling companions to do this for you. This is very important since it will establish a direct line of communication between a doctor that knows you well and the primary care physician treating you in the host country. Determinations can then be made as to what procedures need to be done immediately and those that can wait. Once you know the details of your injuries, determine a course of action based on the least amount of care that can be done in the host country, weighed against the length of time it will take to get back to your own doctor.

The reason we say this is because some medical procedures, if done improperly, can have lifelong implications. If you can get back home fairly quick, then it may be best to wait on some procedures. Robert Pelton can attest to this based on his experience with his motorcycle accident in Peru. After returning to the States, he had to undergo reconstructive surgery to repair not only the effects of the wreck but also the effects of the host country's medical work.

It is very important to keep a first-aid kit on your person at all times, even when traveling in cities. This kit should have your personal medications as well as basic wound care items. First-aid kits will be discussed in detail in Chapter 10, but one thing that needs touching on here is the importance of carrying your own needles and syringes. In the Third World this gives added protection against contracting all sorts of diseases should you need an injection. Simply tell the doctor to use your own gear instead of whatever they have at the facility. This has become a fairly widespread practice among travelers, so it's doubtful you will hurt anyone's feelings. Even if it does, I would rather bruise someone's ego than suffer the possible alternative.

Although we have made out Third World hospitals to be nothing more than M*A*S*H units, remember we are talking about the worst-case scenario. Even in developing countries, the larger cities typically have competent health care facilities. Nonetheless, if given a choice, always try to get home to handle everything except absolute emergency care.

Once medical services have been rendered, payment will be expected before you leave the hospital. If your insurance does not cover you, that payment will have to be made in cash or possibly with a credit card if the facility accepts them. The only consolation is that medical costs are cheaper in most Third World countries than in the United States, and you may even be able to bargain the price down. In the event you do not have enough money to settle the bill, you should have a stash of backup money in the United States that you can draw from. If worst comes to worst, contact the U.S. Embassy and ask them to get involved in the bargaining process. This may or may not work, but it's worth a try.

Finally, before you set off on your great adventure, contact the nonprofit organization International Association for Medical Assistance to Travelers (IAMAT). You can join for a minimum donation, and it provides reference materials for travelers and lists English-speaking doctors in every country that is a member of the organization. The member doctors' primary goal is to provide better health care to those visiting their country and help simplify an already complex situation. They can also assist the traveler in making payment arrangements or arranging medical evacuation to the United States.

CHAPTER 6

Social Life:
The Good, the Bad, and the Ugly

We've talked about a lot of ugly things that can ruin your trip, but we know you didn't travel all this way to be a hermit in your hotel room. As long as you remain aware and keep your wits about you, there's no reason not to enjoy what the country has to offer. We've hauled clients overseas who were literally petrified to open themselves up and enjoy a trip. They did fine in the backcountry and working through a mission to reach an objective, but put them in the midst of a social atmosphere and they froze up. I suppose everyone has their idiosyncrasies, but you have to unwind and kick back every once in a while.

Adventure travel is a work hard/play hard scenario, and the Third World lends itself well to this. The indigenous folks in these areas are some of the hardest-working folks you will ever run across, but make no mistake about it— they like to enjoy life when the day is done. Many of them can outparty, outdrink, and outdance any American I know, and if you're an American with some cash to blow, you won't be short on friends to help you spend it.

NIGHTLIFE

Nightlife in the Third World can be like living a *National Geographic* story, only better. You not only get to see the new sights but also the sounds and smells that fill out the experience. It can be a lot of fun if you use some common sense; it can turn disastrous if you don't.

On one of our trips, our group spent the last night in a small Third World city we often frequent. Breaking our rule of always staying together, one of the guys decided he was going to split off on his own and take a rickshaw taxi back to the hotel to change clothes. Unfortunately, he didn't know the language or how to navigate through the city. Since it was already dark, just about everything he had seen during the day was now unfamiliar to him. The rickshaw driver took a different route to his hotel than he had traveled previously and our guy got nervous, thinking the driver was going to take him somewhere and rob him. Our guy weighed about 250 pounds and the driver weighed all of 90 pounds. Since he didn't speak the native language he couldn't communicate his concerns, so he pulled a Rambo knife out and held it at the driver's throat, screaming at him in English to take him back. The driver stopped and let him out before proceeding to the police. We had to do a lot of apologizing to the local police and military to smooth it over. (This same guy had a bit more to drink later, ended up with a transvestite in his room, and refused to believe another team member who tried to inform him of the gender of his guest. To quote the warden from the movie *Cool Hand Luke*, "There are some men you just can't reach.")

The nightlife and party scene in the Third World is a step back in time. Walk into a nightspot and you'll wish you'd worn your bell-bottom pants and gold chains. I've been to clubs and juke joints all over the world, and all of them seem to have the same American disco music pumping energy into the crowd, the same dim lighting, the same disco ball sparkling rainbows of light on the dance floor, and the same party atmosphere. If it wasn't for the DJ speaking in his native language, you would think you were in the United States reliving the 1970s.

Typically, none of the clubs really get going until just before midnight, and then the party goes all night long or at least until they cut the power off in the town. On one of our trips into the Andes, we had driven most of the night and finally decided to rent a hotel room. The only place we could find cost $5 a night but was located over the only dance club in town. After two hours of tossing and turning to the bass beat vibrating through the floor, we finally went downstairs and joined the party until dawn.

If you visit a club that's rocking away with '70s disco and loud techno music, don't be surprised when the girls asks the men to dance. These folks love to dance and have a good time. If you are shy or worried about embarrassing yourself, just remember the rule we live by in these situations: "Have a good time because you'll probably never see these people again."

A warning is in order here. If you decide to find a woman to enjoy the night with—whether it's dancing, dining, or making love—be aware of the potential problems. Many women may be married and out on the town without their husbands knowing it, or they could be single but with a steady, jealous boyfriend. Even if there is no attachment, many Third World men get pissed when they see a "rich American" cavorting with their local women. If these types of problems crop up, the safest advice is to walk away as fast as possible. Don't allow pride and alcohol to force you into a fight. Trust me, it's much better to go home alone than it is to wake up in a Third World jail.

Some of the smaller establishments can be great if you want to talk to local people one on one and practice your language skills. Don't be surprised if you get pressed into service when things get busy. We had spent a lot of time in one small hotel bar and grill and got to know the owner and employees pretty well. When a group of about 30 people flooded the place and began ordering food, the employees couldn't handle it all. We ended up serving our own drinks as well as those of some of the customers, running our own bar tab, and busing tables for the waitresses. After the place was cleared and the dishes were washed, we had a good time dancing with the waitresses and partying with all the regular clientele.

No matter what kind of club or bar you go to, it is wise to go in a group or at least in a pair. Drinking alone presents you as a prime target for a thief or scam artist, and your one set of eyes may not be able to pick up on the fact that you are being watched. This is especially true in larger cities. Contrary to what some believe, you do not get smarter the more you drink.

Before you go out, take precautions to conceal your primary money stash, and only use your decoy wallet or spare money wad in public. If you travel very far from your hotel to party, have the front desk clerk write the address of your hotel down on a piece of paper and keep it with you, or simply grab one of the cheap business cards that you'll find at the front desks of many establishments. Then you can show it to the taxi driver later and he will know exactly where to take you since he will not be able to understand the pig Latin you will likely be speaking after you've had too much to drink. Hopefully, one member of your group will remain relatively sober and remember the way back to the hotel.

Even with the bad economies in the Third World, casinos seem to flourish there. Some are nothing more than a few slot machines set out on a dirt floor, while others offer all the amenities of Las Vegas. About the only difference between the two is that Las Vegas has new cars that players attempt to win, while some of the Third World dives offer prizes ranging from electric washing machines to bags of food. Unless you have cash to throw away, we suggest staying totally away from them and living by the rule of never playing another man's game. If you must gamble, stick with the casinos located inside the better hotels. They usually have increased security and refuse to tolerate any bad elements known to frequent such places.

PROSTITUTION

Prostitution is not necessarily limited to dark street corners and brothels, and not all prostitutes are looking to be paid in cash for their services. A client we took to South America struck up a friendly relationship with a waitress at a restaurant we frequent in a particular town. Despite our warnings, he took her back to his hotel room and spent the night with her. The next afternoon as we sat around having a beer, we asked him if he used a condom. He said no, and when we asked him why not, he replied, "Because she's not a whore!" When asked how he knew she wasn't a prostitute, he said, "Because she didn't charge me anything!"

Having sex with any girl in the Third World is like play-ing Russian roulette with the gun cylinder half full of bul-lets. Some of the prostitutes might be discerning, but most are not. The vast majority of the women who come on to foreign men in the Third World are only in it for the money or a ticket out of poverty. The bad part about it is that many are encouraged by their families to find a "rich" American and do whatever it takes to get married and hauled to the States. Once they gain U.S. citizenship and get a grasp on being self-sufficient, they sometimes dump the dirty old man and find some young stud, or they arrange for their boyfriend back home to come to the States. I know this sounds cruel, but sadly it's reality.

On the other hand, we have many American friends who have brought women home from the Third World and been happily married for many years, so in the end your odds of staying together are probably about the same as they are anywhere. Just be careful if you choose to have fun with the local women because the HIV/AIDS virus is thriv-ing in underdeveloped countries. If you must buy compan-ionship, bring your own condoms and use them, and never believe that it is the girl's first time just because you're not being charged. (Oh, I forgot to mention that our friend who "didn't get charged" spent the remainder of his trip cash on a new wardrobe for the waitress.)

Most Third World countries have laws against prostitu-tion, but due to their economies of desperation the laws are ignored. In reality prostitution is widespread and even openly advertised. In countries where it is legal, like Costa Rica, there will be an age limit. The saying there is "16 will get you 20," meaning that if a man gets caught with an underage girl, she will get a slap on the wrist for having no license and the guy will go to jail, the maximum sentence being 20 years. Even in developed countries such as Singapore, prostitution is rampant. You can't chew gum in the city, but you can have a different woman every night if you're so inclined. Having spent several months there, I quickly noticed that just about every bar you walk into has girls lined up waiting for a man to buy them a drink and discuss price. This racket is usually run by the cops and bar owners, who receive a kickback for their pimping service.

MIND-ALTERING SUBSTANCES

If you are ever in the Amazon Basin jungle and have the overwhelming desire to see Walt Disney World in Florida, just hire the local medicine man or shaman to cook up an ayahuasca ceremony for you. A concoction is made from the ayahuasca vine and a few other poisonous plants and administered in an elaborate ceremony to produce visions of the spirit world. It is in fact a strong hallucinogen mixed with a purgative. If you don't have a built-up tolerance for the drug, as the shaman does, you usually vomit it up to keep it from killing you. One small cup of the liquid will act on your central nervous system in about 45 minutes. Then the walls will melt and Mickey and Minnie Mouse will come out and dance with you. Then again, you may have the worst experience of your life. It does not affect everyone the same, and I've seen a few people completely shrug it off after vomiting the liquid up. It has been described by some as a spiritual experience and by others as the worst acid trip they ever had.

If you participate in any ceremony and ingest a mind-altering drug, never do so alone. Once you succumb to the effects of the drug, you are totally vulnerable to the whims of others. Always have a few friends along who are just watching to take care of you if things get out of control. A friend of ours was totally disoriented and would have disappeared into the jungle on such an occasion had we not been there to forcefully stop him. Just be sure your friends are good friends, because participants in an ayahuasca ceremony have been known to get violent during their trips. Having personally participated in these ceremonies on several occasions, we don't recommend them to most adventure travelers.

Author Jeff Randall works with an Amazonian
shaman preparing ayahuasca for a ceremony.

The tropics, and the Amazon jungle in particular, are
full of plants that contain mind-altering substances. It takes
a very knowledgeable and experienced shaman or guide to
know how to prepare them for use. Without proper preparation, the drug might not work and it might even kill you.
These drugs have been part of the religions and ceremonies
of indigenous people for centuries, and they usually frown
on doing it for the sheer fun of it.

Some people use these substances as an aid to exist in their demanding environment. The people of the Andean countries in South America have chewed coca leaves for thousands of years in order to live and work more easily in the thin air of the high mountain climate. Coca leaves can be bought in most remote Andean villages and, when chewed with a special clay, produce extra bursts of energy. They don't use it for recreation like people who snort or smoke processed cocaine in the developed countries.

Other Third World countries have their own types of accepted mind-altering drugs. Alcohol and marijuana are found just about everywhere. But know that some drugs are legal while others are not, so be damned sure you don't ruin your trip with an arrest just because you wanted a short-lived high. Whatever you do, never trust any guide or unknown person off the street who claims he can get you contraband drugs. Their loyalty is sold to the highest bidder, and many times they work for the local cops to frame tourists in order to acquire their cash. It's okay to party, but never allow your partying to jeopardize your security or freedom.

TOURIST ATTRACTIONS

Remember the fun things you wanted to do and see on your adventure? These things are probably what got you interested in going on your trip in the first place. The well-known attractions, festivals, and shopping are undoubtedly a big part of any trip, but keep in mind that you might find these things in a different locale than you thought. You've heard about Cuzco and Machu Pichu, the famous Incan cities in the Peruvian Andes. They are the main tourist draw for Peru and are known all over the world. Well, imagine how surprised we were the first time we climbed up a mountain in northern Peru to see the ruins of another city called Kuelap and discovered it was bigger than Machu Pichu. It contains the ruins of more than 400 homes, some temples, and a stone wall more than 60 feet high that surrounds the entire city. It was even a greater surprise that we were the only ones there.

The lesson is to be flexible with your expectations and scheduling, and once you're in-country ask your guide about local attractions that might be off the beaten path. You will be transported back a thousand years visiting these places and watching these people celebrate and live their everyday lives. The experience you will have and what you will learn from remote peoples and places will be worth more than anything you can see or buy in the popular tourist spots.

If you want to find authentic souvenirs that are not made for tourists, have your guide take you to where the indigenous people shop. There are markets where quality goods are sold either in consignment-type shops or by the makers themselves. Some of these places are located in questionable parts of town, so don't go alone. Getting a taxi back out of this part of town might prove difficult, so it's wise to pay the driver to wait for you. As always, pay him only after his services are finished.

Negotiating a price (otherwise known as haggling) is usually expected in these markets, so don't be too quick to pay the first price you are quoted on something. While you don't want to get ripped off, don't get too bunged up about letting the guy beat you for an extra quarter or dollar or whatever the case may be. He needs it more than you do. On the other hand, don't pay $5 for a piece of fruit because you feel sorry for someone.

Negotiating a price with Third World vendors is fun and very much a part of the cultural experience. If you do it right, it's one of the easiest ways to break the ice with local people. We always walk up with a smile on our face, look around the shop or stall, settle on something of interest, and ask "how much" in the local language. After their reply, we grin big and come back with a funny remark that implies they're asking too much. Almost always the vendor will laugh and start talking to us, because he or she knows that we are enjoying our experience in their country instead of being a typical foreign sourpuss who's only thinking about how cheap they can get something from what they consider to be a "low class" street person.

Negotiation is also an excellent way to increase your language skills and knowledge of the host country. Many of our memorable sideline experiences in the Third World began by talking with street vendors. Once you buy something from them, they open up and willingly give suggestions on interesting places and people. They have an immense amount of knowledge about their area not only because they live and work there but because they talk to dozens of other locals on a daily basis.

If you visit a remote village, be sure to take some trade items since money may not be of use to them. Again, a good guide can tell you what to expect and what the remote people will want. Their standards for trade goods are usually very specific, so forget about T-shirts, tennis shoes, and "trinkets." Many of them need working tools or materials for their daily livelihood. We traded with the Urarina Indians of South America many years ago, and they would accept only scissors, fishing line, fish hooks, certain color beads, and red cloth (red was the only color the women were allowed to wear). When buying or trading, be careful that you don't acquire something prohibited to take out of the country or back to the United States by import-export laws. What is legal to possess inside the host country may be banned for international export, period.

While visiting some of the remote areas, ask your guide about any yearly festivals and if outsiders are permitted to attend. If you can coincide your visit with such an event, it is well worth it. Festival and party time in the Third World is absolutely wide open. There is nothing like line dancing to a monotone, three-piece band with a dozen feather-headdressed, bare-breasted women after drinking a quart of spit beer. It's a crash course in learning about and *living* a new culture and its customs.

Just about any Third World country has indigenous tourist attractions.
This tribe of Indians in South America caters to tourists by
performing traditional tribal dances and music.

If you are lucky enough to be in-country during a festival period, it's usually a lot safer to attend those in smaller
villages than the ones held in larger cities. Large festivals
will bring out the partygoers but also attract every thief and
con artist for miles around. The big festivals are fun, but stay
on guard and make sure you keep all money and documents secure and well hidden. That's why we usually party
in the smaller towns, where we can drink all night with the
local police and stay out of trouble.

In general, remember that tourist areas are a haven for petty criminals, beggars, and con artists. If you want to see the real country and what it has to offer, seek out the unknown real-world settings. Good guides can get you into places far more interesting than the country's museums and tourist junk shops. Why look at a display in a glass case when you can see it in its natural state, face-to-face? Looking at pre-Colombian art in a fancy building is great, but seeing it extracted from the ground in its raw state is an awesome experience. Who wants to sit on a nonsmoking, air-conditioned tour bus with little blue-haired ladies when you can hitch a ride with Julio in his Volkswagen Beetle and scream through town with the Rolling Stones blaring on the radio? Adventure travel is about experiencing the true culture of a country, so enjoy yourself, get to know the people and town, and bring back the stories an average tourist will never be able to tell.

CHAPTER 7

Going Bush

Once you leave the confines of the concrete jungle and wander off into the real jungle, the whole adventure scenario changes. Having lived in wilderness settings for weeks at a time, we prefer them over more civilized surroundings due to the absence of man and his fast-paced world. Once you get the hang of it, it becomes somewhat comfortable living within the parameters of your pack and what the wilds provide. I could give you the typical romantic lines about "finding one's self" or "getting close to nature," but the truth is that the wilderness offers us a grown-up's playground to do things that are out of sync with normal life.

Think about it. When you're at home, how many times do you get the chance to tromp through swamps, catch alligators, eat snakes and lizards, build thatched shelters, take a dump in a hole in the ground as fire ants sting your ass, battle bugs and mosquitos, and wonder what the hell is crawling up your leg in the middle of the night? Oh, and the best part is sitting around the campfire in the evenings bragging and laughing about all these manly deeds.

I admit that extended stays in the bush also make me thankful we humans were intelligent enough to build dry houses with indoor plumbing; invent the automobile, television, and heaters and air conditioners with thermostats; and come up with the concept of McDonald's restaurants with drive-thru services! But people these days have become accustomed to living within their own comfort zones, never feeling secure enough to leave the world of Wal-Marts, cable television, and fine restaurants. The biggest challenge many of us ever face is finding the remote control before the Sunday football game kickoff.

Some of us strive to break this cycle by turning to activities such as expeditions and extreme adventure. The allure of testing yourself in unknown environments and seeing firsthand how the rest of the world lives are probably the main reasons we do it. It's also a good feeling to know you have the knowledge and experience to survive in these conditions if you were ever forced to.

Team members on a Randall's Adventure & Training expedition
practice jungle living skills in Latin America.

An extended bush stay has a way of bringing out the
worst in even the most sweet, innocent, and forgiving person. The tiring and often boring nature of expeditions will
often shorten tempers and eventually infect every traveler
with momentary bursts of assholism. If you're wondering
whether you and your girlfriend have the ability to get married and live happily ever after, take her on a hard bush
expedition first. If you walk out still holding hands and

worrying about the other's comforts before your own, you'll be married forever.

Even with all the tiring work and hardships associated with expeditions, there's something about bush life that's addicting. You bushwhack until you're ready to puke, haul boats over sandbars and through thick jungle, pull enough vehicles out of the muck to qualify for a Land Rover commercial, eat things that would make a billy goat regurgitate, live in mud and water for days at a time, and finally get so damned tired of seeing wilderness that you could scream. But once you reach your goal, light up a cigar, and take a long slug of the brandy you've been saving, you feel like the king of the world. That's when you realize everything you have endured over the past few weeks has been worth it. Those moments are what make life worth living. Of all the clients we have hauled to the bush and all the bitching and moaning we have heard while there, not one of them has ever said "I wish I had never done this" after it was over.

Dealing with the serious bush is a bit of a mind game. Good bushmen are those who can reach a certain level of insanity while in the wilderness—not some crazed, knife-between-the-teeth Rambo mentality, but a hunger for adversity, thus a hunger for adventure. Those who enjoy pushing the envelope do so because they love to test themselves. They reach down deep inside themselves and find that extra strength that sometimes goes beyond the body's physical ability to endure. They don't complain about a lack of proper gear or an abundance of hard work to reach an objective. They do it for the challenge and learning value. They refuse to quit even when confronted with the hardest adversity.

Surprisingly, some of the best clients we have taken to hard bush have been unassuming city folks who have never ventured much into the backcountry but have a true desire for adventure and testing themselves. The worst have been boisterous military types who claim to have no fear and like to brag and lie about all their supposed skills and secret covert special operations work, then end up whining and bitching the whole trip. Without fail, they're always selfish with their gear, obsessive at keeping things from crawling on them, first to eat, and dead last when it comes to getting dirty and helping the whole team. Every adventure always has at least one of these macho men, and we have found that when they're tasked with a simple bush skill they usually fall short. Typically, they blame their shortcomings on their fellow teammates or improper gear. Their favorite excuse is, "Well, this is not the way we did it in the military."

Once you go bush, everything you've ever known about day-to-day life changes, and every part of your meager existence becomes a chore. If your head is screwed on too tight it will finally get to you. As trip leaders on numerous expeditions into the Third World bush, we have dealt with panic attacks, fights between clients, sickness, injury, and several other emergencies that were caused by mental distress. During our adventures, we have learned to be mother, doctor, psychologist, friend, and sometimes drill sergeant just to keep the trip on track.

The best advice for anyone deciding to join an extremely remote adventure is to relax, learn to laugh at yourself, and take every minute, every hour, and every day as it comes. Just about any serious expedition will consist of 90 percent boredom, 5 percent fun, and 5 percent terror, with a lot of cursing and nervous laughter in between. Gear will break down, schedules will go to hell, and problems you never dreamed of will crop up, but it is life and adventure at its finest level.

SURVIVAL KITS:
PERSONAL WILDERNESS INSURANCE

The best insurance policy for any adventure traveler is to be self-sustaining anyplace, anytime, anywhere. Survival kits will help you do just that.

Many times when traveling in the bush, you will leave

your main pack at the campsite, on the boat, or in the vehicle while you take a short side trip. Yet the very time you leave your vital gear somewhere else is the time you may find yourself needing it. So take the time to build a small kit that will become a permanent part of your body until your travels are finished. It is a last-ditch tool to be used when nothing else is available and an emergency presents itself.

Kits can range in size from an Altoid tin stuffed with bare-bone necessities to backpacks stuffed with tents and emergency rations. It all depends on your skill level, the environment you're traveling in, and what you're comfortable with if you find yourself in a survival situation. We suggest building a kit that covers the following survival necessities: fire, shelter, water, navigation, and the ability to gather food. For most climates, all of this gear will fit comfortably in the large front pockets of a travel vest.

For fire starting, pack a small ferrocerium rod (an alloy of iron and cerium used for lighter flints), two Bic lighters, a package of water-resistant matches, a couple of first-aid alcohol prep pads, and a few military surplus Trioxane heat tablets. If you can't find Trioxane, there are other fuel tabs available on the commercial market. If you want to make your own, coat cotton balls in Vaseline and stuff them in a 35mm film canister. These will light and burn even after being submerged in water. With these few lightweight components and the skills described in Chapter 9, anyone can start a fire under any weather condition.

For shelter we suggest packing a small space blanket, a couple of contractor-grade garbage bags, and 50 feet of parachute cord or similar cordage. If you don't mind the extra weight, include a military-style poncho. I've spent many nights sleeping comfortably in the jungle under a poncho shelter. They also make a very good warming blanket for those suffering the effects of cool weather.

Water requirements are for purification and gathering capability only. Iodine-based water purification tablets such as Potable Aqua or a liquid form called Polar Pure are good first-line defenses, but they are ineffective against some waterborne problems. If you are allergic to iodine, there are several companies marketing chlorine purification tablets that work well, but they too may be ineffective against certain problems.

The ideal water-carrying device is a collapsible container such as a CamelBak water bladder. These not only work for holding water but they can also be blown up and used as emergency personal flotation devices. Cheaper containers include large zip-lock plastic bags and condoms. A condom packs up small and will expand to many times its size. If you ever have to use one for a canteen, use a sock as a protective wrapper, which will keep it from rupturing easily. Once it's filled, tie it off with a small piece of cordage. Never try to tie it like a balloon because it will break when you attempt to untie it.

With one exception, the food portion of your survival kit contains no food. Instead it has lightweight tools to help you secure food. A fishing kit with a few hooks, a small roll of line, a steel leader with swivels built in, several lead sinkers, and several pieces of field corn for bait can be used for fishing or making simple hook snares for small game. As an emergency source of quick calories, we throw in a couple of beef bouillon cubes. Taking up very little room in your kit, the bouillon makes a quick meal when boiled in water and provides a large amount of calories in a good-tasting broth. The cubes also make good bait for fish and animals.

If you have the room, the best survival fishing device is a gill net. A standard 4 x 12-foot net is about the size of a small fist when rolled up. It also comes in handy as an improvised shelter because the weaving is ready to accept large leaves or other vegetation for a roof or side walls to protect against the elements.

Navigation survival tools are used for situations when you need to self-rescue and hike out of the bush. A good baseplate compass with sighting ability, pencil, waterproof notepad, and a set of "ranger beads" (a string of counting beads used to record distance traveled) will allow you to walk a straight line and draw a map of your route should you need to return to the spot you started from. Signaling devices should also be a part of the navigation portion of your kit, including a rescue whistle, good signal mirror, aerial pencil flares, and small pieces of reflective tape. The tape can be used to mark your camp for ease of finding should you walk off in the night, mark a riverbank where potential rescuers may be shining lights searching for you, or placed anywhere that would reflect a searcher's light.

Miscellaneous components of your survival kit should include a large sewing needle, a small roll of thin stainless steel or brass wire, a multitool or similar folding knife, and two sources of light. A Mini-Mag flashlight with extra batteries works well, and the new long-life LED (light-emitting diode) mini lights are superior tools for the bush.

Wilderness survival kits can be purchased commercially or built a piece at a time directly out of the local Wal-Mart camping department. Again, we suggest lightweight travel vests for expeditionary or international travel because they provide an easy way to carry all of these items on your person at all times. In contrast, bags and packs are not always going to be on the traveler's body and are susceptible to loss.

However you decide to carry these tools, just remember that the most important part of any survival kit is having it securely on your person at all times. It has absolutely no value sitting beside you in the seat of a boat (unless it is in a waterproof container doubling as your emergency flotation device, as previously discussed), in the back of a car, or in the bottom of your pack. If the boat capsizes in the middle of the night along some lonely stretch of river, you will probably not be able to grab your kit before being dunked. The same thing goes with traveling in a vehicle. What's to say that you won't have to make an emergency exit and haul ass to avoid gunfire, or what if you get separated from your companions as you stop to take a leak along the side of the road? Some folks might think this sounds paranoid, but the items above require very little space and weigh very little for the return on the investment. Build your kit, seal the components in plastic zip-lock bags, stow them in your pockets, and don't use anything from it unless it's an emergency. If you do use parts of the kit out of convenience, replace the items as soon as you can.

For those of you without any wilderness survival training, there are several pocket survival guides available that take up very little room and make for interesting reading around the camp. *The Collins Gem SAS Survival Guide* is slightly bigger than a pack of cigarettes and covers the full spectrum of wilderness survival, navigation, and rescue in every imaginable climate and terrain. We consider it a valuable addition to any survival kit for travel adventure.

METHODS OF TRAVEL

Expeditionary travel is reverse industrialization at an accelerated pace. You board a multimillion-dollar jumbo jet as you leave the comforts of your civilized home, arrive at an international airport in a new land, and from there what you think of as civilization progressively decreases until you're miles away from anything that even resembles your life a few days earlier. Once you start into the bush there's no such thing as luxury transportation. Except for a possible bush flight landing on a drug runner's discreet airstrip or dirt runway, most of your movement into the inner depths of a country will be via junk vehicles, boats, rickshaws, motorcycles, your own two feet, and maybe a few pack animals thrown into the mix. The mechanical options are inevitably held together with baling wire and rely on ingenuity and luck to keep moving.

Of all the things you do in the Third World, transportation always pans out as being the single most culturally diverse, the most fun, and the most dangerous event in the whole adventure. So have your affairs in order and cash in hand because the locals will take you to the top of the

Rivers are the main transportation avenues and means of living in most tropical areas. Small dugout canoes and wooden boats are used just like automobiles in the United States.

mountain or the inner depths of the jungle, but it's done their way, and they don't take American Express. You have stepped into a world with few enforced laws or regulations. The name of the game is to use whatever works at the time to haul tourists, terrorists, rebels, locals, chickens, pigs, or any other cargo to their destination, whether separately or all at once.

In tropical regions, rivers are the major source of moving everything from point A to point B. For many remote locations, small canoes, rafts, and wooden boats are the only transportation options for tourists as well as those who live there. So don't be surprised if your adventure lands you and your gear in the middle of an overcrowded death ship chugging across a river seemingly the size of the ocean, or taking a shortcut through the middle of a swamp.

As many times as I have been in the middle of the mighty Amazon River, it still amazes me to watch a huge barge chug by just inches from a fisherman in a dugout canoe. No life vests, no running lights, no safety equipment—nothing but a small, leaky canoe carved from a tree hauling one or two people and a fishing net more than a mile from shore. Of course the locals think nothing of it. Why should they? They've been doing things the same way for thousands of years, and they're not going to let progress stand in the way of making a living.

If you're looking for cheap river transportation between port towns, check to see if the waterway has a ferry system. Every adventurer should subject himself to at least one multiple-day ferry ride in the Third World. It's an unforgettable experience, with standing room only amongst a cultural cross section of people. There are beautiful women, ugly women, little folks, and big folks. Multiple races and languages will be represented. On some ferries there are even jail cells for transporting criminals. It's like a Third World bus ride on steroids, except there's not enough breeze to hold down the stench. Chickens, cows, goats, and people all share the same rusty deck with diesel engines churning the beast ever so slowly up the river. Usually there's only one bathroom that's nothing more than a hole in the floor, dumping all the waste directly into the river. When nature calls, you'll see a lot of folks just hanging it over the side instead of dealing with the bathroom. Once the ferry gets close to port, some folks will jump over the side and swim to shore. (I never have figured this out. Either it's just for fun, or they're just damn glad to be free of the ferry.)

Vehicle rides in remote areas are not much different

from those in the cities, except the roads are rougher and can be much more dangerous. Breakdowns are a common occurrence, and typically the vehicle is worked on in the travel lane or left there until someone tows it out of the way. But surprisingly, it's probably safer traveling in these parts than it is in a major U.S. city. One thing we've noticed is a common courtesy among Third World drivers—if you can call it that. Sure, they love to blow their horns and curse the driver in front of them, but there are very few cases of road rage. If Americans tried some of the stunts we've seen pulled on the Pan-American Highway, a gun would be drawn and shooting would commence.

It is also a generally accepted practice to pick up hitch-hikers. We've started out on many adventures in an over-packed minivan, only to add more people and animals along the way. Most of the areas we're talking about are very remote, so hitchhiking is the only way the local populace has to travel into town to pick up supplies.

Using whatever form of transportation is available to get away from the city is the only way to travel to most remote destinations. If you can keep from worrying and accept the lack of physical comfort for a while, it will probably become one of the more memorable experiences of your whole trip.

DANGERS OF REMOTE TRAVEL

Although the backcountry holds a lot of potential danger, in our opinion it's a lot less dangerous than most of the cities you will travel in. The greatest concerns of traveling through the wilderness are diseases and infections, having a medical emergency without being in close proximity to a hospital, getting lost, and problems associated with the weather and natural disasters.

Hollywood and television have probably done more to scare the hell out of hard-core adventurers than this book will ever do. Many supposedly true documentaries will have you believe that bushmaster snakes have a seek-and-

This is the real world when it comes to hunting snakes, not some TV crocodile hunter BS. During the capture of this 20-foot anaconda, our guide sustained a nasty bite on his leg.

destroy attitude toward humans, piranhas lie in wait for unsuspecting gringos to wade through their river, and an alligator's favorite meal is a wilderness adventurer. It's bullshit, plain and simple, the professional wrestling of the documentary world.

The least concern you will have in most wilderness and remote areas is the animal life. For the most part, those creatures that live in the wilds, including the dreaded poisonous snakes and grizzly bears, will steer clear of you if given a chance. Shows such as "The Crocodile Hunter" have ruined the public's perception of these animals. In fact, it's very difficult to walk into any wilderness and readily find snakes, alligators, or bears without actively searching them out. In a truly wild environment, many of these creatures have a natural fear of man and head in the opposite direction when approached. What the public doesn't see on TV is all the set-up shots of placing the snakes or other beasts in certain locations to be "found" later by the famous host.

Only after you place your feet on the forest floor can you truly understand that the wilderness is not at all like a zoo. To see many of these animals takes patience as well as good guides. To be attacked by these animals is a long shot. You are much more likely to be struck by lightning than die in the jaws of some nasty beast. Of course if you decide to part with common sense and approach a bull elephant protecting his herd, impress your friends by sticking your head in a croc's mouth, or ride a hippo like a piece of rodeo stock, you will probably die. On the bright side, the world will be much better off without your genes in the reproductive pool.

Another aspect of Third World travel that receives a lot of hype is terrorists and rebels. No doubt there are folks out there who will kill you just because you looked at them wrong, but you don't have to leave home to find them. If you follow the advice in this book, you will most likely be viewed as another nonthreatening tourist who has no value on the kidnap or burial market. I'm sorry to tell you this, but you're just not that important to most folks. Ruling out a "wrong place-wrong time" scenario, if you do end up in an area where people kill people for sport or due to hatred of a nationality, you obviously didn't do your pre-trip research, or you were actively seeking danger to prove something. Never go searching for anything you are not prepared to handle—you just might find it.

Our friend Robert Pelton has traveled all over the world interviewing every type of rebel and bad guy that can be found, and as of this writing he's still alive and living comfortably at his house in California. Some folks call that being

Photos of a Contra base camp in the mountains of Nicaragua. The American adventurer Bill Johnson lived and worked here for many months supporting their fight against the communist Sandanista government. (Bill Johnson photos)

lucky; we believe it's because he has an ability to communicate with honorable intentions, remain neutral, and, most important, have a complete understanding of the mission and dangers before trekking into the land that time forgot and really doesn't care to remember.

Weather and natural disasters should always be looked at as potential dangers when traveling the backcountry. Some areas may be prone to severe flooding or snowstorms, raging forest fires, devastating mud slides, and a whole host of other threats that may occur with little or no warning. Always research seasonal conditions and the long-range forecast for a region before traveling there, and keep your eyes open for safe zones and improvised shelters as you travel.

Weather probably rates as the number one accidental killer in the wilderness. There have been numerous documented cases where lightning has killed climbers and hikers taking shelter on rock faces or under trees. If you're caught in a thunderstorm, take the lowest position you can find and shed aluminum-frame packs, canoe paddles, or anything else that will make you more attractive. If you're traveling with a group and get caught in an open area, always separate yourself from the rest of the crowd. Huddling together makes a bigger target and will kill the whole bunch if lightning strikes.

Be extra careful traveling on muddy mountainous roads after hard rains because mud slides are commonplace on underdeveloped infrastructures. Also take care around any waterways since rain can swell creeks, rivers, and lowlands to deadly levels in just a few minutes. During one of our rope training classes in Central America, we had several clients on rope at the top of an 80-foot waterfall. After delaying our descent due to a short rainstorm, we proceeded down the rock face to find a raging torrent of water below. One of the first climbers to go off rope was huddled against a narrow ledge when I reached the bottom. As he moved out of the way to make room for me, the water caught him and swept him to another waterfall dropoff.

Of all the dangers posed by remote travel, none are greater
than the microscopic threats. This village water supply is a
prime area for contracting a whole host of diseases.

Luckily, I grabbed him by his harness just as he was about to go over, saving him from a 40-foot fall into the flooded waters below. After the whole team was safely at the bottom, we rigged a Tyrolean traverse to get everyone across the flooded creek and back on the trail to camp.

Once you are wet, hypothermia can be a serious threat, even in tropical environments. Some of the coldest days we have experienced have been in Third World locales near the equator. Shoving rafts for hours down a jungle stream or riding in a boat up the river with rain pounding on you can lower your core body temperature quickly. Once your body starts shivering, then it's time to find a way to regain heat. We will cover how to treat hypothermia under wilderness conditions in Chapter 10.

Of all the potential dangers posed by harsh wilderness environments, the microscopic ones are the deadliest. Waterborne viruses and bacteria are major concerns in any developing country, as are a lot of other medical conditions such as hemorrhagic fevers, rabies, and a whole host of other nasties that the United States and other developed countries pretty much have a handle on. Until good prophylactics were invented, malaria killed more people worldwide than all the major wars combined. Even with such drugs as Lariam and Doxycycline on the market, there are still strains of malaria that are resistant to them, so as with all potential bugs, prevention is the best medicine.

Using common sense, practicing sound personal hygiene, and researching the possible dangers before you travel will go a long way in keeping you healthy. Doing your best to keep mosquitos from biting you, in conjunction with taking preventive medications, is a lot better than taking a chance and treating the infection after you're sick. Purifying your drinking water is preferable to doing a dose of Flagil to remove the parasitic infection from your gut. Avoiding people who are obviously sick is better than trying to figure out what you have once you return home.

CHAPTER 8

Proven Gear for Extreme Environments

There is a small rodent common to the Western U.S. called a packrat. It hoards anything and everything it comes into contact with, presumably because it thinks it will need it for something. We have had several clients who put the packrat to shame by bringing more "stuff" than is physically possible to cram into a minivan. It's simply amazing to sit back and watch a whole Wal-Mart unfold in front of your eyes as they unload their packs. They always have every gadget, snack food, article of clothing, and piece of gear that the largest outdoor supplier would carry, but somehow they forget essential items such as first-aid supplies and their common sense. These travelers always have a couple of things in common: They have done very little research, and they always leave trip preparations until the last minute, then buy everything in sight thinking they might need it— just like the packrat.

Even if you're not a packrat, choosing the wrong gear or low-quality equipment for a trip to an extreme environment will cost you. During one of my first trips to the South American jungles, a teammate brought along a pop-up tent of the type seen in the movie *Congo*. The only set-up required was to loosen a strap, throw the tent in the air to let it uncoil, and presto, you had a tent ready to crawl in. Of course we ribbed him about the tent, but after the first couple of nights in the jungle he was laughing at us. Every night we slaved to set up mosquito nets and waterproof tarps while he was already snoring inside his pop-up tent.

But his gear failed him in the end. On the third night we all took a canoe ride to a local village and ended up drinking cane rum with the villagers until late in the evening. After returning to camp, our drunken pop-up tent camper zipped himself inside his tent and, as luck would have it, a large nasty-looking spider had managed to crawl in with him. Needless to say he went ballistic, and in his hurried state he managed to jam the cheap zippers on the tent trying to get out. Of course the rest of us were laughing our asses off as he threatened to kill all of us for not helping him. Finally, we heard a loud ripping sound as our friend emerged through the top of the tent, put his knife back in his pocket, and decided to spend the remainder of the night in an Indian's thatched hut. The sliced-up tent was given to the Indians the next day, and our friend spent the rest of the trip sleeping under a mosquito net and poncho like the rest of us.

For the most part, essential gear will be dependent on the environment in which you have chosen to travel. The two questions we usually ask about clothing and gear before carrying it on a trip are (1) will it work, and (2) what does it weigh? A tool that works will do you no good if you have to be a pack mule to carry it. Conversely, there are a lot of good gadgets that are light and easy to carry but simply don't work in extreme environments.

Proper packing for any trip is a combination of destination research and common sense. For most temperate to tropical climates, we carry proven wilderness adventure gear that we have used time and time again in our travels. We design our pack load to be less than 40 pounds (excluding camera gear) in order to maintain our rule of self-sufficiency and mobility. With our system we can easily travel through international airports, cities, and steamy jungles, and we can stay warm even while bivouacking overnight 12,000 feet up the Andes.

The following is a rundown on basic gear we have used for adventure travel, along with its positive and negative attributes. These are merely guidelines and thoughts based on our experience; the authors make no commission or profit from their inclusion in this book. In the end, travelers should draw their own conclusions as to what they will need for their own trips.

CLOTHING AND FOOTWEAR

There is a long-running debate on cotton versus synthetics for clothing and fabric-related gear in the bush.

Cotton has been the traditional choice and is still most widely used by the indigenous people in underdeveloped countries, but remember it is usually grown locally and is therefore cheaper for them to acquire. Cotton has also been the choice for people with allergies to a variety of other fabric materials. In the last few years, however, synthetic clothing has been developed that more closely mimics the soft, comfortable feel of cotton, and it is far superior when it comes to drying quickly and weighing less.

In tropical regions, staying dry when traveling can be a serious problem. You want water to be wicked away from your body and your clothes to become dry as quickly as possible, which is exactly what the new synthetic materials do. Wearing cotton socks that refuse to dry out can result in foot diseases that have the potential to stop your travels. Even underwear is better when made of fast-drying synthetic. (About the only thing better is no underwear at all.)

Any cotton clothing that gets wet will become heavier and add to your pack load. Even the multipocketed travel vests we absolutely depend on when traveling overseas weigh a ton when wet, so be sure to pick one that's made of a synthetic material instead of cotton. And this doesn't apply only to clothing—if you've ever picked up an old cotton canvas army tent after a night in the rain, you know exactly what I'm talking about. Fortunately, most tarps, ponchos, packs, and tents are now made from much lighter synthetics that also take up less room when packed.

Even hot climates can cool off at night, so a light, water-resistant jacket with a hood can help knock the chill off, but we suggest military style ponchos due to their ability to be used as shelter or rain gear. These tightly woven nylon ponchos do not "breathe," so they hold body heat in, keeping you warm. Several times I've been soaked to the bone and cold yet immediately felt warmer after pulling a wet poncho around me. There is also a liner available for military ponchos that works well and doubles as a blanket in cooler climates.

About the only cotton gear we suggest for extended travels in tropical climates are your city street clothes (some travelers prefer going with synthetics for city wear, and that's fine—it's a personal preference), bandanas, and any hat you might wear. A cotton hat will keep your head cooler when it's wet, and a damp bandana around your neck makes bush travel much more comfortable.

Color can be an important factor when selecting clothing, packs, or any other gear you carry into remote areas. A lot of adventure clothing and gear is available from military surplus outlets, but keep in mind that camouflage is not a good choice. If terrorist or guerrilla forces see you in camouflage in the bush, they might assume that you are regular military and thus hostile. Result? You'll be shot. If the regular military sees you, they might assume you are terrorist or guerrilla personnel and thus hostile. Result? You'll be shot. Choose lighter, solid colors whenever possible. Lighter colors don't absorb as much heat from the sun, and there is some research from the Center for Disease Control (CDC) that suggests lighter colors don't attract mosquitos as much as darker colors.

The one piece of gear that can totally ruin your trip is your footwear. This is particularly true when it comes to boots for cross-country hiking. In the jungle no boot is waterproof, so forget about the $250 high-tech marvel boot. They become water buckets when you step into soup up to your chin. The boot of choice for a wet, jungle environment is the Vietnam-style jungle boot made by Altama. It has drain holes near the bottom to let water escape and a Panama sole which grips mud better than most. It also has a high upper which will protect you from biting, stinging insects and plants with needles.

Beware of the imitations that go for about one-fourth the cost of Altama boots. Without exception, every pair of these cheap boots I've seen go into the jungle fell apart before the trip ended. Be nice to yourself and get decent boots.

You should also take a lighter pair of shoes for walking in the city and other times when you are not actually in the bush. These can be light hiking shoes or tennis shoes that are easy to stuff into a pack. This second pair is also great for walking around camp after being in wet boots all day. The current crop of sport sandals are okay, but they do not give the foot any protection from the side, especially in jungle environments. River shoes used by rafters are great, but their specific function doesn't make them suitable for every hard bush activity, and their construction makes them tear easily in bush camps. It is not advisable to go barefoot like the locals because you don't have the thick callused soles they do, and even the locals are susceptible to bites, stings, and sharp needles on plants, not to mention broken glass and rusty pieces of junk that might be lying around.

PACKS

Hiking through dense vegetation is always livened up when someone's large, moving-van-sized pack smacks an overhanging tree limb and stirs up a nest of hornets or wasps. Large packs of 5,000 cubic-inch volume capacity or more are just too unwieldy to carry in dense vegetation. Not only do they get caught on every tree and vine you pass, but gear ends up buried in the middle of the cavernous main compartment, making it difficult to keep organized. We have found that packs with a volume capacity of 2,500 cubic inches or less work better for bush travel. If you're really good, you can do like most indigenous military personnel and carry a very small day pack filled only with the bare essentials and derive everything else from the environment.

Internal frame packs work best because they keep the weight close to your back where it belongs, and they don't get caught on vegetation as much as external frame packs. The external frame will allow ventilation between your back and the pack, but the tradeoff isn't worth it when you get into dense vegetation or are trying to load it on a city bus. In the latter case, the frame has a tendency to get hung up in other folks' gear, and because the pack cannot be compressed, it cannot be pushed down into smaller cracks, which is sometime required to get all the baggage on a crowded bus. With any pack, it's a good idea to line it with a plastic trash bag before putting gear in it to keep its contents dry. (You should do this even if your pack is advertised as waterproof.)

The best pack we've come across for adventure travel is the Becker Patrol Pack designed by our friend Ethan Becker. Ethan has spent years developing gear and survival techniques for extreme environments. The Patrol Pack carries well, is built like a tank yet is small and light, and will accept an internal water bladder for hydration as you hike. It has plenty of tie points for external gear and several small compartments to keep the rest of your stuff organized and easily accessible. Once you learn which compartment you keep a particular item in, it is easy to find even in total darkness. It carries just as well through the city as it does in the bush, making it an ideal choice for adventure travel.

Whatever pack you choose, stay with synthetic material construction for its strength, and choose a dull, muted color. If you have to carry your pack through town, you really don't need a bright pack to advertise you like a neon sign as a tourist. Here again, stay away from camouflage color schemes.

SHELTERS AND SLEEPING GEAR

Cheap tents and hammocks have only one redeeming quality—they can provide much-needed humor after a hard day of hacking through the bush. During a filming venture for the Travel Channel's "Ian Wright's Amazing Adventures" series, one of our teammates from England spent a considerable amount of time setting up a poor-quality hammock before retiring for a night's sleep. Sometime in the middle of the night, the cheap nylon began to come

Well-built gear is an absolute necessity for extended stays in harsh environments. Here, Jeff Randall, wearing a Becker Patrol Pack, helps a soldier set up a radio during a training session with the Peruvian military.

apart with a series of resounding rips before depositing its occupant on the floor of a mosquito-infested swamp in his underwear. Half an hour later, aided only by our howling laughter, he managed to rig the failed hammock into a shelter in the muck on the ground. He didn't sleep that night, but he did make a large blood donation to the local mosquito population.

Having a quality tent, tarp, and ground cloth is important not only for the practical aspects of staying dry and sleeping well but for the psychological value of providing a quick haven from the rain and insects. These three pieces of gear should be light, durable, and of good overall quality.

When choosing a tent, select one from a well-known manufacturer that is easy to set up (after all, you may have to set up a campsite in darkness during a heavy downpour) and has enough room to sit up in and store a bit of gear inside with you. I've carried a two-man North Face tent that will go up in about five minutes. A good, waterproof ground cloth underneath keeps the moisture from coming up through the bottom.

To complete your shelter requirements, get a good quality tarp about 10 x 12 feet in size and weighing 6–7 ounces. It will cost about $60, but it's worth every penny. Hang it up and you've got a shelter under which you can set up two tents or one tent and a lot of gear. There are cheaper tarps that are of good quality, but they weigh a lot more and don't pack up very small.

Hammocks and one-man bivouac sacks (or "bivys") are light and small but leave no room for gear or an extra occupant in an emergency. Hammocks do provide the psychological advantage of getting you off the forest floor away from the critters, but they take longer to set up than a small tent and are confining to sleep in. Another problem with hammocks is that your feet end up higher than the rest of your body, resulting in poor circulation and numb feet come morning. Try sleeping in one before you take one to the bush.

In tropical climates, bivys are nothing more than hot-house torture chambers that allow zero room for equipment, not to mention they're a bitch to get in and out of with muddy feet and clothes. Even though they tend to be extremely waterproof and lightweight, in our opinion they are useless for tropical travel.

If you choose to forgo the tent and use a mosquito net/poncho-style shelter, make sure it's a quality military net made from a synthetic material and a quality full-size military poncho. The meshing on many of the cheaper nets is too large and does not keep out the smaller insects. Cotton nets, although tightly meshed for insect protection, are extremely hot and uncomfortable to sleep under in tropical conditions.

Whatever shelter you choose, always make sure it has enough room to store your shoes and clothes inside with you. Leaving any clothing outside overnight attracts a whole host of biting visitors looking for a sweaty place to rest.

Another piece of gear we always travel with is a Therma-Rest mattress. These are invaluable for keeping the ground from sucking heat from your body's core and helping you sleep just a little more comfortably on hard ground. Most of these are self-inflating by simply opening the valve and waiting on the inner foam to suck air in and expand (carry a small repair kit in case a puncture is sustained). They also make great cushions for extended travels in the backs of trucks or the hard seats of Third World boats, and they can be used as emergency flotation devices in a pinch. We carry the three-quarter length version, which rolls up compactly to 4 inches in diameter by 8 inches long. For extended stays in a bush environment, they are well worth the money.

Sleeping in tropical locales requires no sleeping bag. It sometimes gets cool in the mornings, but a simple poncho is sufficient to keep you warm. If you're wet before going to bed, we suggest drying off before retiring and sleeping naked (except for socks and a hat). Sleeping fully dressed usually leads to sweating and a restless night's sleep. A padded sleeping area, poncho, hat, dry socks, and a makeshift pillow will assure most anyone of a comfortable night's sleep.

The bottom line with shelter and sleeping arrangements is to always have a quality setup. Unless you are on a wilderness training expedition that requires you to live on the minimum, then having the right gear for comfortable sleep is one of the most important ways to safely reach your adventure goal. Work and play hard during the day, but always get a good night's sleep when the day is through.

KNIVES

Of all the tools necessary for extreme wilderness environments, sharp steel rates at the top of the list. In most environments, a good knife is the one tool that has the ability to provide you with shelter, water, food, navigation, and, when used with the proper technique, fire.

Now just because a knife is considered a priority survival tool doesn't mean you should spend your life savings to acquire one. Many "survival" knives have about as much hype attached to them as a Tom Brokaw news story, so beware. Many custom models will do no better in extreme environments than a proven production model. In fact, during one of our military training trips we carried several custom jungle knives built by a well-known manufacturer. Three days into the trip one of the knives bent like a wet noodle when it was applied to a heavy chopping chore. The cheap machetes had to finish the job.

The type of knife you need is dependent on the area you plan to travel. Knife manufacturers nowadays seem to build their products for prying bulldozers away from oak trees, yet the thick blades and heavy grinds do nothing but add pack weight and drastically reduce the knife's ability to cut. If you're a first-time knife buyer/user, avoid these altogether and concentrate on more efficient, common-sense designs.

For most wilderness, a sheath blade with no more than 5 inches of edge length and the ability to sharpen easily will work just fine. We prefer flat ground knives with thin edges and no serrations, which are useless in this environment because they use up a major portion of the knife's edge. Most combination edges (plain/serrated) have the serrations toward the back of the blade, where a lot of the actual cutting occurs. As a result, cutting efficiency is drastically decreased. Sure, serrations are fine for heavier canvas and rope, but a properly sharpened straight edge will work just as well. It's also a lot harder to sharpen serrations than it is plain edges.

Some "survival instructors" claim that tanto or other "tactical" point designs are best for the wilderness, but in our opinion these instructors are more interested in selling their product than providing sound information about tough outdoor blades. Knives with "belly" in the blade (a pronounced rounded curve of the cutting edge near the blade point) provide a much more efficient means of separating hide from game, dicing up camp food, and performing other common camp chores, and they are easier to sharpen. If you don't believe this, walk into any slaughterhouse and look at the knives the butchers are using.

Avoid the new, overrated mystery steels that sales hype claims will cut forever. Simple carbon steel has been cutting and killing in the Third World for eons. Sure it will rust, but who gives a damn if your blade looks bad as long as the edge is sharp and it fills its role as a tool. This is not to say that many of the stainless steels are no good; just that the drastic increase in price hardly ever justifies the slight increase in quality. Instead of spending your money on one expensive knife, buy a couple of good cheaper models. If you break one, then you have a backup.

Besides cutting efficiency, the only thing we really require on sheath knives is a good-fitting handle, especially if the expedition is knife intensive where a lot of bush has to be cut. Poor handles will create hot spots and blisters that don't heal well in wilderness environments. One of the best handle materials is Micarta in either the canvas or linen grade. It grips well when wet, is impervious to powerful insect repellent like DEET and other chemicals, and heat or cold doesn't affect it. If your trip requires working around a lot of water, be sure to attach a safety lanyard to your knife and use it; otherwise a simple slip of the hand will sacrifice your primary survival tool to the River Gods.

The best deal for your money in an all-around outdoor knife is a standard military-issue Ka-Bar fixed blade or its equivalent. These are a little longer than our suggested 5 inches, but for their low price they are as tough as nails, hold a good edge, and sharpen easily. We've used these time and time again under adverse conditions and found that they're just like the Energizer bunny—they keep going and going. Another good line of knives that we have used and abused in the wilderness comes from Becker Knife & Tool division of Camillus Cutlery. They are extremely well-made and practical, and the company offers everything from camp knives to machetes.

Back up your fixed blade with a good multiple-use folder like a Swiss Army Knife (SAK) and you're ready for whatever the wilderness throws at you. One of the better models of SAK is called the Rucksack. It features a very efficient folding, wood-cutting saw that is valuable around camp for cutting small saplings, building shelters, cutting bones, and a thousand other uses.

Whatever you do, avoid the Rambo-type survival knives, especially those with saw backs. Every one we have ever used has been useless in the wild, and the saw back actually decreased the usability of the knife since it interfered with splitting kindling wood with a baton (i.e., small cut of wood) on the spine or when beating the knife through a small sapling when snap cutting. They also hurt your hand when used in draw-knife fashion while peeling bark for cordage material or skinning poles—something we do a lot in our wilderness travels.

If we had to choose only one blade to survive in any environment, it would be a machete. Machetes are pure survival tools. They have an edge thin enough to bush-whack through thick second-growth vegetation, and they are versatile enough to cut large trees, make shelters, kill alligators, dress game, and even give you a secure handhold when going up muddy banks or climbing trees. For the money (about $15 for a good one), no other tool can out-perform it for survival type work. They're also one hell of a good defensive weapon. We would safely assume that just about as many folks have been killed with a large machete-type blade over the years as by gunfire.

If your pack size and weight can accommodate it, buy an Ontario Government Issue machete and you'll be light-years ahead of the rest of your traveling companions with their $200 survival knives. If you want a small knife to pair up with a machete, consider something along the lines of a quality kitchen knife such as an Old Hickory brand. Small paring knives are invaluable around the camp and typically are very efficient, easy to sharpen, and don't set you back a whole lot if you lose them.

If you're willing to spend a little more money for a quality machete-type blade ($79 at the time of this writing), then check out the knife designed to conquer everything from harsh jungles to family campgrounds. Named the RTAK (Randall's Training & Adventure Knife), it is now a production knife manufactured by Ontario Knife Company. We designed this blade after years of tweaking and finding out what works in the real world. It combines the quick slicing capabilities of a machete with the comfort and usability of a sheath knife. RTAKs are being used all over the world by military personnel (including the prestigious Peruvian Force Jungle Survival School) and drug eradication teams operating in heavy wilderness conditions, so one will work just fine for the demands of adventure travel.

Knife sheaths are more of a personal preference than anything else. For extended stays in humid environments, it's best to avoid leather and opt for synthetic materials such as Kydex, Concealex, Nylon, or Cordura. If you're going to be using a machete for most of your travels, a simple piece of duct tape placed over the edge does a good job for transportation. Once you hit serious bush, your blade will usual-

For temperate to tropical climates, nothing beats a machete. Brian Horner, instructor and owner of Learn To Return Survival School, works with a machete while a military officer oversees his progress.

The Ontario RTAK designed by Randall's Adventure & Training is
the authors' idea of a perfect adventure-travel survival blade.
This design will handle any bush task efficiently.

ly be carried in the hand, thrown in the bottom of the boat, stuck in the ground, or stored in a pack, so sheaths are not that important. All you want is something to carry your knife securely while keeping it from cutting anything it's not suppose to.

For wilderness knife sharpening, we use multigrit diamond hones. These are very lightweight, take up little space, and sharpen like crazy. When sharpening machetes for tropical work, try to thin the edge out so it cuts vegetation easily. If most of your work will require heavy chopping, then less thinning of the edge will decrease the problem of the blade sticking in the cut.

If you have no sharpening device, flat rocks such as sandstone work very well. To get a good sharpening surface, rub two flat rocks together, adding water as you work them back and forth. This will flatten the stones and produce a decent area for sharpening most knives.

Anytime you sharpen, always add water as you stroke the knife. This induces micrograin breakdown and cleaning of the sharpening stone, thus producing quicker and more even results in your sharpening. Another point that needs to be made here is to forget about perfect edge angles. If you look at any indigenous knife—or for that matter any farmer's pocket knife—it's usually sharpened very thin because the end result cuts better and is a lot easier to resharpen.

NAVIGATIONAL AND ELECTRONIC GEAR

There is one word that has the potential to cause instant panic during adventure travel, and that word is "lost." You could be in a triple canopy jungle with no view of the sky, in a deep canyon surrounded by rock walls, in an open desert with total overcast skies, or in the middle of a large city surrounded by tall buildings. In all of these situations you cannot see the sun or stars or far-off landmarks to orient yourself. Fortunately, a simple $10 baseplate compass made by a reputable company will get you on the right track after you learn a few basic techniques on how to use it. You can also spend between $30 and $50 for a mirrored compass, which will enable you to do more precise navigation and provides a means to signal a potential rescuer if you are in trouble.

When buying a decent compass, always look for one by such reputable makers as Brunton, Nexus, Suunto, Recta, or Silva. We've tested various models from all of these manufacturers and had great luck with them under harsh conditions. Second, look for a baseplate or mirrored model that has a see-through base so it can be used on a map to orient yourself and determine your route. Third, the compass should have a liquid-filled capsule that is waterproof. Some of these models will have a feature for magnetic declination adjustment that is needed for precise navigation and large-area navigation, but a small baseplate without this feature is fine for work in a small area.

Of all the compasses available, we prefer the Silva Ranger as our primary direction-finding device. There are also electronic compasses that still operate off the Earth's magnetic field but use batteries to provide a digital readout for direction as well as other data. Corsica, Suunto, and Outback produce good quality units that are waterproof and tough, although extreme cold can affect the digital readout and battery performance.

The most popular electronic device to hit the outdoor market in the last few years is the global positioning system, or GPS. The popularity of the GPS is due to its ability to access information from a network of satellites, record coordinates of many positions along a route, and show your position anywhere on the face of the Earth within a few feet. Brunton, Magellan, Lowrance, Suunto, and Garmin all have various models on the market, but the technology is evolving so rapidly and prices continue to fall so fast that it is impossible to definitively recommend a particular brand or model here. For the record, we've carried Garmin,

Magellan, and Lowrance GPS devices into extreme tropical environments with varying success. Of all of these, the Lowrance GlobalNav 212 seemed to have the best reception and battery life.

Navigation with a GPS requires that three satellite signals be locked before your position can be acquired; failure to lock on at least this many signals renders the device useless. Because they work from satellite signals rather than the Earth's magnetic field, their main Achilles heel is a blocked signal that prevents them from receiving information. Anything from severely cloudy skies to buildings and dense vegetation can cause this, although a GPS will work most of the time. To overcome reception problems, always go with a 12-channel model.

No GPS or electronic compass completely replaces a simple, basic compass. Electronics are dependant on batteries that can fail, and there is nothing as reliable as the magnetized needle of a simple compass pointing the way. If you are using a GPS in an area with poor reception, a magnetic compass is required because the internal GPS compass may not give you immediate coordinates when navigating to safety.

The best combination is to have a good quality GPS coupled with a reliable compass and the knowledge to use both. This way you can navigate anywhere, in any condition, with precision and reliability.

CAMERA EQUIPMENT

Whether you're a professional photographer or just making a record of the trip for yourself, the basic problems with cameras are the same. Heat and water are the two natural elements that cause problems for cameras and film, and the tropics offer the worst of both. High humidity and heat will cause film to get slightly sticky, causing the camera motors to work harder. We've had a few inexpensive point-and-shoot cameras die in the jungle because of this.

We started using a high-quality, water-resistant point-

and-shoot that solved most of the moisture-related problems. We can pull this camera out in the pouring rain to get a photo and not worry about it. Just know that the point-and-shoot cameras are fine for snapshots, but they are severely limited for higher quality photos because you cannot change lenses or filters.

For the average photographer, we suggest taking at least two cameras. One should be a more expensive SLR (single lens reflex) for high-quality images and the second a small, water-resistant point-and-shoot for quick offhand shots or photos during inclement weather. For most SLR work in the wilderness, a 28-105mm lens coupled with a circular polarizing filter is perfect.

Cameras, electronic gear, and flashlights use a variety of batteries, so one trick is to buy your electronic gear so that each piece uses the same size battery. Of course this is almost an impossibility for SLR and video cameras (which require specialized batteries), but flashlights, GPSs, and other common gear can be matched for battery size. It's much handier carrying several packages of AAs than packing along various sizes.

On extended bush trips, a small solar battery charger is a valuable tool to prolong the life of your video camera and charge other necessary batteries. Having a charger also keeps pack weight down because you don't have to haul as many batteries. If you are using any type of recharging device, buy metal hydride batteries. They're expensive on the front end but will not hold a memory like other rechargeable batteries, meaning you can recharge them when they are at half power, three-quarter power, or zero power and get their maximum energy value every time. This makes life a lot easier if you only have a little bit of time to soak some juice in them.

We carry our more expensive SLR cameras in a camera bag with lenses and accessories, and the whole bag goes in a dry-seal bag when rain hits or we do water crossings. Putting a desiccant chemical in with the camera gear doesn't work well in a tropical environment because it becomes waterlogged in a very short time and then only becomes dead weight.

MISCELLANEOUS GEAR

Miscellaneous gear is defined by us as items that are not absolutely required to survive but sure make life better if you have them along. As with the major gear discussed above, the type of miscellaneous things you take along will depend on the environment and activities your trip entails. Some adventures will require specialty gear to complete the trip safely, a typical example being a mountain climbing expedition, where ropes, ascenders, rappelling devices, and other technical tools would be needed.

There is not a enough space in this book to cover every type of outdoor adventure gear, so we will touch on common items that have been found to be useful during most expeditionary travel. The best advice when gearing up for an adventure is to think logically about what you will need to complete your mission. If you have done your pre-trip research, then this should be easy and will most definitely save you from the "packing the kitchen sink" syndrome often suffered by newcomers to this activity.

Water Filters

"If you go there, don't drink the water" has been said of most of the Third World and at least half of the industrialized nations on Earth. If you've ever spent a night or two hanging off the back of the boat feeding the catfish, you can appreciate the importance of that advice. Indigenous people have developed immunities to many of the waterborne bacteria that cause visitors like us to get sick. Simply put, you risk getting diarrhea and other ailments if you drink the water without treating or filtering it first, and diarrhea, if unchecked, can lead to dehydration, a potentially life-threatening condition.

Fortunately, ceramic-cartridge water filters are inexpensive, small, and easy to use. MSR, Sweetwater, Katydyne, and Pur filters have all made many trips with us and perform well in most situations. Make sure the model you get is capable of filtering out Giardia and cryptosporidium, which can cause serious illness if you ingest either. In fact, always buy a water filter that is guaranteed to trap any particle larger than .3 microns so you are assured of removing crypto cysts. You should be able to filter one gallon of water in five to 10 minutes depending on the water quality you start with. Most good filters will cost between $50 and $80, and replacement cartridges are readily available at outdoor stores.

Although ceramic-cartridge filters are the best means of purifying water, they do have limitations. To date we have not found a small hand-held filter that will work in black water—water in creeks, rivers, or swamps that has a brown to black color due to a high content of dissolved organic matter such as tannic acid. The filter cartridge will typically clog before it will provide a quart of water from one of these sources. You can break down the filter and clean the cartridge, but doing this for about three days to keep up with just one person's water requirements will render the cartridge unusable when it wears beyond a certain point.

There are companies that produce filters that will not clog in black water, but they do not remove some of the smaller particles that ceramic cartridges will eliminate. No prefiltering (including coffee filters) will remove the small organic matter that clogs the filter, so we have been experimenting with "floculants." When applied to black water, this ingredient traps the small organic matter in a suspension and then sinks to the bottom of the container, leaving clear water. This can then be pumped through a ceramic filter without the clogging problems. Currently, this product is not available on the civilian market, but initial tests look promising and it may eventually win Food and Drug Administration (FDA) approval for normal consumers.

When water filters fail due to extreme situations, such as becoming clogged with black water, you had better have a backup plan. Iodine or chlorine tablets and boiling are viable options if you do not know where and how to obtain drinkable water from the environment you are in. Iodine-based products such as Potable Aqua and Polar Pure have been proven effective against waterborne problems such as Giardia but are not guaranteed to work against cryptosporidium spores. Some people are severely allergic to iodine, so chlorine is the next best thing. Chlorine takes a little longer to treat the water and, although not guaranteed to eliminate every waterborne problem, is a generally accepted means of purifying water, thus the reason for its widespread use in most municipal water systems.

We carry both iodine and chlorine tablets as a backup for our water filter. If we're dealing with a highly questionable water source, we use both a chemical agent and the filter or simply boil the water for a foolproof method, which is why we always have some type of pot as part of our adventure travel gear. The pot also works well to prepare fresh game into soup to gain the full nutritional value from the catch (the cooking broth contains much of the food's nutrients).

Cooking Gear

There is a golden rule concerning food in wilderness areas: "If you can't peel it or cook it, then don't eat it." We've bent this rule at times by eating a few crawling critters off the jungle floor, but in general it's a good rule to cook most things first.

If you want to carry a portable cook stove, be aware of two things: the availability of fuel in your travel area and the extra pack weight the fuel adds. It is illegal to carry fuel in luggage on an airplane, so you'll have to acquire it at your destination. The multifuel stoves, therefore, are the best choice because you can burn about any volatile liquid in them, including the hooch you brought along to share with the locals. Due to realistic space limitations in your pack, you are only going to be able to carry a quart or less of fuel in the bush, so look for a stove that burns fuel economically. This usually translates to one that has a good variable temperature range. Some of the stoves on the market either burn very low or wide open, with nothing in between. The low temperature doesn't cook well or boil water quickly, and the wide-open burn expends more fuel than is needed to cook.

If you spend a lot of time in the bush, it's probably wise to learn how to build a cook fire from materials in the surrounding environment and forego carrying a stove or fuel. This is the option we most often use since the areas we travel in don't restrict the building of open fires. More on this important skill in the next chapter.

If you must opt for a stove, consider a simple alcohol stove such as the lightweight Trangia or equivalent. These work fairly well, take up little pack space, and are very conservative on fuel, and you can legally carry fuel for them on an aircraft by taking along a bottle of any drinking alcohol that has a 100 proof or higher rating.

Lights

Flashlights will probably eat your batteries faster than anything else you have. If you have a solar charger you can keep a fresh supply of batteries available, but it's better to use your light sparingly to start with. People tend to overuse their light sources mainly out of insecurity and fear. It's dark and you're in a totally foreign environment, so naturally you want to see what's out there when night falls. Yet we've seen indigenous people leave a campsite at dusk to set traps and scout for game, return, then go out again after midnight and come back at daylight with game—all without a light of any kind. Understanding and getting familiar with the environment you are in will make you more comfortable, and you'll find yourself using your light less and less.

In tropical regions a bright white light can actually be a

detriment around the campsite. It will draw every nocturnal biting and stinging insect right to your camp, adding to your misery and discomfort. The best route is a red or blue colored light around camp and a white light for long-range observation.

A small flashlight such as a Mini-Maglite is fine for a main light source in just about any wilderness. It is water-proof, which is a main requirement for any light since it will be used rain or shine and for night water crossings. Mini-Mags also have a candle feature that works by unscrewing the lens cap and placing it on the bottom of the flashlight as a stand, allowing the bulb to burn continuously just like a candle. This is extremely handy when working on chores around camp at night or as a reading light inside your shelter. Whatever main light source you choose, be sure to carry a spare bulb.

We also use headlamps on our trips. They provide excellent light directed toward your field of view while freeing your hands to set up camp or do other chores (we use them for hand-catching snakes and alligators for food or study). Most headlamps (such as our preferred model, the Princeton Tec) utilize AA batteries, which are the same size used in most GPS units and all Mini-Maglites.

To supplement your main light source and to conserve batteries, get a small, inexpensive micro-LED light such as an ASP or photon light. It will provide illumination only in your immediate area, but most of the time that's exactly where you use a flashlight. Micro lights come in a variety of colors, including white, red, and blue. The colored LED lights are best because they do not cause temporary night blindness when you turn them on. This is particularly useful if you need to rummage through a pack in a boat to find something but you don't want to interfere with the boat driver's vision since he will probably be driving with no lights at all. A low-intensity blue light is also useful if for some reason you don't want to be seen from a distance. The biggest advantage to these small lights is that they have a virtually indefinite life span. This is mainly due to their momentary switch, making it impossible to leave them on for extended periods. Keep one clipped to your vest or belt loop and you will rarely pick up your main light source.

Multitools

For their size and versatility, multitools are probably one of the best inventions to come along for the adventure traveler. Whether you are in the city or wilderness, there will be a myriad of situations where this compact tool will come in handy. We have used multitools to repair rental cars, patch up boat motors, fix electrical outlets, open beer bottles, and pull large slivers of wood out of a gentleman's hand.

Gerber, Leatherman, SOG, and a lot of other well-known manufacturers are making high-quality, compact multitools. Whichever one you choose, make sure that it has a decent saw blade, a straight edge knife blade, a good can opener, a bottle opener, pliers, and a straight and Phillips head screwdriver. With these few tools, you can make repairs in remote locations that might not have been possible otherwise.

We prefer the Gerber because their long-nose pliers version seems to be more user friendly for various situations. It works well, for instance, when extracting hooks out of a fish mouth or holding small game or fish for cleaning and dressing chores. As a side note, the long-nose model would make a good compact defensive tool when gripped in the strong hand with the pliers pointing downward. It definitely wouldn't attract as much attention on a crowded city street as walking around with a knife on your belt or clipped to your pocket.

● ● ● ● ●

We could get into many other pieces of travel gear if space allowed. A lot of it boils down to personal preference, though. For example, when I travel to the tropics I carry no mosquito repellent because mosquitoes have never been attracted to me. Other travelers have to carry 100 percent DEET repellent just to find some temporary relief. If you'll be traveling to high altitudes or sunny climates, strong sunscreen may be a necessity, whereas it might be considered a luxury item elsewhere. Gear repair bits such as nylon thread, needles, duct tape, and cordage are not absolutely required for survival, but they can be stowed in relatively small spaces and would certainly be appreciated if something needed mending. Of course, a lot of these things may already be covered in your survival and first-aid kits.

A good idea is to lay out all of your gear on the floor before you leave and break it down into major categories to make sure you have everything covered. Food, water, fire, shelter, navigation, first aid, rescue, and travel documents are the categories we always look at when preparing for a trip. You must think carefully about the variables within each category. For example, navigation requires being able to know direction, relating direction to the environment, and then executing your determined route in reality. What would be required to perform this task in a remote environment? Ask this question to an inexperienced traveler and the typical answer will be "a map and compass." But what about flashlights to travel at night if the need arises, or a watch to judge time traveled, or some type of device to measure the distance traveled? Or how about the simplest of items: a paper and pencil to take notes, record bearings, and draw rough maps as you travel? The secret to picking the necessary gear is to look at the big picture, then break it down into the "what ifs." If you can do that logically, then you will cover yourself for most situations without overpacking and becoming a walking Wal-Mart.

CHAPTER 9

Real-World
Wilderness Survival

Since there are already enough books, articles, and videos on the topic of wilderness survival skills to fill a city library, in this book we are only going to touch on the basics. The following techniques and tips have been acquired directly from our travels and have been applied by the authors time and time again in hard wilderness. Most of them pertain to tropical and subtropical environments, but they can be applied over a wide range of environments. What you are about to read will be extremely beneficial to you should you ever find yourself in a wilderness setting facing a life-threatening situation.

In order to be proficient at anything, you must practice, practice, and then practice some more. The problem with practice is that it's almost always done in a controlled environment. For example, I have known a couple of black belt martial artists who ended up in the hospital because in the real world some drunken redneck caught them with a "lucky" punch or a fortunate beer bottle. The same goes for wilderness survival. I'm probably as proficient a primitive fire maker as you will find, but put me in a new environment in a downpour of rain and I will mostly likely have serious difficulty starting a fire by friction or with true flint and steel, if I succeed at all. So although reading books, watching videotapes, and practicing in the wilderness is fine, knowing "it's just practice" in a controlled environment is always enough to allow an unfair advantage.

Although any learned skill is a valuable tool to the wilderness adventurer, no situation will ever present itself as the survival books explain it, including this one. To be blunt, you cannot "learn" survival no matter how many books or videotapes you study. An instructor can only enlighten you to the methods that aid in various types of wilderness skills. Although you may eventually master these procedures, you still do not know what your exact survival requirements will be until you are faced with a real situation. It can be as simple as running away from an immediate threat, such as a mugger or forest fire, or as complicated as living for months on human flesh as was seen in the famous Andean plane crash in the early 1970s. In all cases, learning about and understanding your environment—as well as yourself—are the key ingredients to personal survival.

The number one question that always pops up from a newcomer to survival skills is, "What do you feel is the most important survival skill?" There is no answer to this because it depends on the particular area and the circumstances surrounding it. If you had just survived a plane crash in a hostile area of Africa, your number one concern may not be food, water, or shelter—instead, it may be to hide yourself from those who may wish to kill you (provided you are not seriously injured). On the other hand, if you were stranded in a remote area of the Arctic, the first priorities would most likely be finding shelter from the elements and building a fire. In the desert? Shelter and water. In a large body of water? The ability to keep your head above the water. Facing a pissed-off sow grizzly bear with your hunting partner? The ability to outrun your companion.

To choose one skill or specialize in one area makes you useful only on the grounds of your choosing. To be a jack of all trades and the master of none takes your survival potential to new levels. Science fiction and survival author Robert Heinlein summed it up real well when he wrote:

"A human being should be able to change a diaper, plan an invasion, butcher a hog, conn a ship, design a building, write a sonnet, balance accounts, build a wall, set a bone, comfort the dying, take orders, give orders, cooperate, act alone, solve equations, analyze a new problem, pitch manure, program a computer, cook a tasty meal, fight efficiently, die gallantly. Specialization is for insects."

In short, there is no one skill that will see you through all survival scenarios, even in the wilderness. There is, however, one trait you cannot afford to be without—a will to survive. Of all the skills that wilderness survival encompasses, none is more important than having an offensive mind-set. Much could be and has been written on this subject, but it has been our experience that mental training is best left to the individual. It has also been our experience that there are those who will never develop this attitude and be nothing more than fodder should an unexpected situation occur.

Simply put, an offensive mind-set is a combination of confidence, aggressiveness, and a die-hard will to overcome adversity even when the odds are stacked against you. Those who truly embrace this mind-set usually enjoy facing adversity for its training value. Maintaining this will to live is without doubt the one element that will see you through any livable situation, whether it's being attacked by a street thug or ending up lost and injured in a wilderness area.

An offensive mind-set should never be confused with ego. The man who dies battling a gang of street thugs just to prove his manliness is stupid, especially if he had the option of running and surviving. An offensive attitude toward survival is never a contest of the strongest, smartest, or toughest. Quite simply, it's accepting the situation and finding the best way to continue living. When you think about it, "survival" is actually a natural human reaction known as *staying alive*. Yet if you do not approach adversity with an overwhelming desire to live at all costs, your chances of survival diminish drastically.

ASSESSING THE SITUATION

The first rule of survival is to not panic. You should always take time to analyze your situation and clear your head before jumping to conclusions.

After you realize you are in a potential survival situation, assess your immediate priorities, meaning those that must be dealt with within the next 24 hours. Believe it or not, most folks are rescued within three days, so keep that in mind as you ask yourself questions about your predicament and weigh the positives and negatives of your options.

Do I need to stop and make a camp for the night, or can I hike out before dark? How late in the day is it? Is there a storm brewing? How cold will it be when night falls? Am I lost? Do I need medical attention? Questions such as these will help you formulate an immediate plan of action.

As long as you're not in need of immediate medical care or some other emergency assistance, your best bet may be to stop, make camp, build a fire, and get a night's sleep to clear your head and rest your body before attempting self-rescue. Do not allow your ego to control your actions. Sure, it's embarrassing to admit you got lost in the woods, but one of the most important rules of wilderness survival is to accept your situation. Don't tell yourself you "screwed up" and proceed to beat yourself up for it. Instead, calm down and accept what's happened, then make a decision based on your assessment of the situation.

Whatever you do, trust yourself and stick to your decision. Never make a decision, prepare to implement it, then back out because you're not sure if you chose correctly. If you have honestly assessed your situation based on facts instead of fear, your gut decision will most likely be the correct one.

FIRE

Of all the wilderness survival skills that can be practiced or acquired, the ability to produce fire rates toward the top of the list. When Tom Hank's character in the movie *Castaway* turned a hard-earned ember into a roaring flame, it was a defining moment for the character as well as the audience. Everyone seemed to know that his survival was no longer a question.

Of course that was just a movie, but the psychology behind that scene was very real. Fire not only cooks your food, purifies your water, and keeps you warm; it also provides psychological comfort. A man who has fire has companionship, thus instilling confidence and the most important survival trait: a desire to continue living.

Building a fire under adverse conditions takes practice. Here, Jeff Randall and his indigenous guide smoke a small monkey taken for food.

In the wilderness, there are three primary methods of fire starting: flame-based (e.g., lighters, matches), spark-based (e.g., ferrocerium rods, true flint and steel), and coal-based (e.g., bow drills, hand drills, pump drills, fire saws). Of all of these, the simple flame-based fire is the most reliable method for most locations. The problem with creating fires this way is the unreliability of the flame source. Butane lighters degrade quickly in cold weather, and once they get wet they're useless until dry. Waterproof matches are good, but the quality of the flame they produce is affected by wind and dampness.

Our favorite backup tool for fire starting is a ferrocerium rod. These come in various sizes, but for ease of use we suggest a 1/4-inch diameter rod about 3 inches long. Made from the same material used in lighter flints, the rod showers a mass of super-heated sparks when stroked with a sharp object. The only downside with ferrocerium rods is that you must have dry tinder or a fuel tab to produce a flame, and they generally require two hands to operate. In a severe hypothermic situation, it may be difficult to make your hands cooperate when attempting to strike the rod.

If all else fails or you have no fire-making devices with you, friction fires are possible. The bow drill is the best method for most situations. The only problem with making friction fires is that it usually take a lot of practice to perform with efficiency, and even at that the materials have to be properly prepared and dried before it will be successful.

Now that we have an understanding of the three forms of fire making, let's look at the process to implement them successfully.

Fire building is a step-by-step process, and preparation is the key to success. The first thing you need to have is a supply of tinder to start the fire. Sources of reliable tinder that will catch readily from a small flame include bird and mouse nests, various tree barks, dead grasses, pocket lint, and some types of dry leaves. In a worst-case scenario, try various items from your first-aid kit to get a flame going. Bug repellent, alcohol prep pads, many ointments, and sipping whiskey are highly flammable.

Another good source for tinder is small dead trees that are still standing. These can be broken down into smaller parts and will be dry inside. Using your pocket knife, whittle "fuzz sticks" from finger-sized pieces of this wood by making a series of small cuts that expose shavings on the stick. You will be able to light these with your lighter. The remainder of the tree can then be used for kindling.

You can also search for "fat-wood," which is old tree stumps, usually evergreens, that have a highly flammable concentration of sap in the stump. Fat-wood will have a distinct smell of turpentine when broken apart. Pine trees are probably the most famous for producing great fat-wood stumps, but we have found flammable resin species of trees all over the world.

Once you have a good tinder bundle, gather progressively larger pieces of wood and have these ready before you even light the tinder. Again, always search for standing dead wood since it sheds more water than dead wood lying on the ground, which absorbs more. The middle portions of standing dead trees will be the driest. You can also chop into dead wood lying on the ground to extract the drier center portions.

If you're going to rely on flame-based fire starters to ignite your tinder, then keep a few military Trioxane heat tabs in your kit. These will light with the weakest of flame or spark and burn very hot in all weather conditions and long enough to ignite even damp kindling wood. At the very least, have a small tea candle that can be lit and slid under tinder to dry it out and eventually catch it on fire. Candles aren't as good as the heat tabs because they have to be protected from the elements, whereas the tabs will work in windy or damp conditions.

The reason we like ferrocerium rods so much is because they work under any condition. It doesn't matter if it's 30 below zero or a monsoon is coming—ferro rods will always produce sparks. Stroked with the back of your knife, a sharp rock, or even a piece of broken glass, they shower a ton of white-hot sparks into your tinder. Used correctly and with minimal practice, they will light most of the same types of tinder that a flame will unless the tinder is damp. In such cases we use the ferro rods to light Trioxane heat tabs, or we'll place a first-aid alcohol prep pad or other flammable substance on the tinder to produce a small fire immediately.

One trick we teach when using ferro rods is to hold the striker (knife, rock, glass, etc.) static just above your tinder bundle and rip the ferro rod backward along the striking edge. This will prevent you from hitting the tinder with a downward stroke and keep the sparks directed into the bundle.

Many companies produce ferrocerium rods attached to a block of magnesium. Scraping a small pile of magnesium into your tinder bundle will light damp tinder, but it is usually more trouble than it's worth because any slight breeze will blow the shavings away, and the magnesium only produces a short-lived flash fire once it lights.

Finally, if you are intent on pulling your best impersonation of Tom Hanks and his *Castaway* character, try your luck with a friction fire. This is something we do not suggest as a survival technique unless you understand the process completely and have practiced extensively. For the average wilderness adventurer, it's much easier to carry several forms of reliable fire-starting gear than to take a chance on friction fire. It is an absolutely last-ditch fire-starting method to be attempted when no other means are available.

Having said that, friction fire is not movie magic. In fact under the right conditions it is one of our preferred methods for starting a fire. We have taught many students how to build fires this way and have recognized it to be one of the biggest confidence builders in the whole spectrum of survival skills.

Choosing and preparing materials is the key ingredient to a successful friction fire. What you want is a soft hardwood for both your drill and fire-board. You're looking for a wood hardness that can be indented with your fingernail. I've used pawpaw, buckeye, cottonwood, yucca stalks, and basswood for boards, and straight pieces of buckeye, horseweed, and the flowering stalks of yucca for drills. Once you have your fire-board material picked out, use your knife to split it down to about 5/8 inch thick and an inch or so wide.

The drill (also called a spindle) should be roughly 1/2 inch in diameter. If you're preparing a hand-drill fire, then the spindle should be between 18 and 24 inches long; for a bow drill it should be at least a foot shorter. After material type, the most important factor to producing a friction fire is to make sure the drill is straight. When you find a suitable piece of straight wood, point both ends of it with your knife for a bow-drill fire and one end for a hand-drill fire.

After all of your materials are gathered and thoroughly dried, use your knife point to create an indentation toward the end of the fire-board in the center of the 1-inch width. The indentation should be deep enough to keep the drill from walking out once the drilling process begins.

For a bow-drill setup, fashion a bow from a springy sapling and cordage. The cord can be anything from your shoelace to natural materials scrounged from your surroundings such as vegetation, barks, and roots that can be woven and twisted into cord. With natural cordage, many times it will take a lot of testing to find something that holds up well to the abuse of a bow-drill system.

The cord is attached to the bow by notching the ends of the bow, running the cordage over both ends and through the notches, then lashing around the notch to secure and keep the material from splitting. The bow should be bent enough to keep your hand from hitting the spindle once the system is in action.

You will also need a cap to provide a bearing surface for the top of your spindle. Very hard woods work well for this; simply whittle out an indentation for the spindle top to rest in. You can grease this area with natural skin oils found on your nose or forehead or with plant and tree resins.

Next, lay the spindle on the cord of the bow and twist it so the cord wraps all the way around the spindle and holds it about halfway along its length. Place your spindle cap on one pointed end of the spindle and place the other end in the socket in the fire-board. Begin drilling into the board by applying downward pressure on the spindle cap while moving the bow back and forth in a sawing motion.

To drill with a hand drill, begin at the top of the spindle and rotate the drill back and forth between your palms as you apply downward pressure. Heating pine or other sticky resins and rubbing it along the spindle will help you maintain a grip. (This resin will also increase the purchase on the cord of a bow drill.) Once you get near the bottom of the drill, hold the drill in the fire-board socket with one hand, move the other hand to the top, and start the process over. When attempting to make a fire with a hand drill, remember to relax and breathe as you work.

Once a definite indentation has been mated between the drill and fire-board with either a hand drill or bow drill, remove the drill and cut a V-shaped notch with your knife extending all the way through the fire-board to almost the center of the indentation. Position a leaf or some other material under the board to catch the dust and coal that will be formed from drilling. Place the board back on the ground with the notch facing away from your body. Step on the board to hold it firmly in place and begin the drilling process again.

As you are drilling, smoke will began to form around the base of the spindle. Keep drilling. Once the dust has built up around the notch, thicker smoke will begin to rise. Keep drilling while increasing downward pressure and rotation speed. Just before you have a coal, heavy smoke will pour from the base of the drill. Give it one more hard and fast pass while tilting the drill toward you slightly to aid in kicking the coal out of the notch.

You will know if you have a coal when you remove the drill and the dust continues to smoke. Simply pick up the leaf and dump the coal into the middle of your tinder bundle. Pick the bundle up head high and blow the flame to life. Use this ignited tinder to start your previously prepared tinder, kindling, and firewood.

Due to book length restrictions, these instructions are very basic. It takes time and practice to be able to consistently produce coals, especially with a hand drill. I have built friction fires in downpours and on humid days with both hand and bow drills, but my materials were preprepared, and I've had plenty of practice with these methods.

For survival purposes, the bow drill will provide you with greater success over all the other friction-fire methods since you can get more power out of it, it saves your palms from bloody blisters, and the increased friction the bow produces has a tendency to dry slightly damp woods.

Another primitive method is true flint and steel. (Many folks get true flint confused with a ferrocerium rod, which is actually artificial flint.) This method uses a piece of hardened steel and a sharp rock from the ground to produce a spark. The only problem with the process is that, unlike with ferrocerium, the sparks produced by true flint and steel are weak, and you must have some type of prepared tinder such as charred cloth or charred wood to catch the spark. For survival purposes, this is not a good technique because it requires an initial fire to char the spark-catching material. It is, however, an excellent technique to practice fire-building skills or as a way of starting other fires after the first fire has been made and tinder charred.

As a side note, be very careful of survival instructors or books that claim you can use any piece of steel to strike against rock and produce a spark capable of being caught in char. This is bullshit in its purest form. Although any metal will produce a spark, consistently making that spark and then catching it in char is almost impossible. True flint strikers are hardened to bring higher carbon levels to their surface. It takes a very hard piece of carbon steel (about 58 Rockwell and above) to consistently produce sparks from rocks found on the ground. Most knives, axes, and other tools are not capable of this because they are heat treated at lower Rockwells for toughness and resistance to breakage.

Finally, magnifying glasses will work to light dry tinder, but many small glasses will not focus enough sunlight to produce sufficient heat. It may be possible in a survival situation to use certain camera or binocular lenses for this process, but it depends on the lens size and power.

No matter which method you use to start your fire, once it is self-sustaining with a good coal bed, wet and green wood will burn in it. Until your fire reaches this point, keep all damp wood standing around or in close proximity to the fire to help the drying process. It may be necessary to build a makeshift fire shelter from large leaves such as palm or fern fronds, dead branches, or the underside of a large log to protect it from heavy rains.

SHELTER

Well, you've finally done it. You managed to come all this way on one pair of clothes, limited cash, a few survival tools, and a good attitude. You have excelled in starting fires for the past few nights and slept under the stars because the weather's been good. Now here you are standing ankle deep in mud with torrential rain falling on your head and nighttime approaching fast. A cold shiver runs down your spine as you think about spending the whole night squatting by a tree in nothing but a drenched rain poncho. Are we having fun yet?

For an initial quick shelter, use your poncho, a garbage bag, or space blanket with some small lengths of parachute cord to make a lean-to. Make this space tall enough to stand under because it will not actually be your permanent sleeping shelter. Be sure to pitch one end so the rain runs off. This side should be on the downhill slope (if there is one) to keep water from running back under your shelter. Once this is set up, go back to your fire-making skills and start a small fire underneath the shelter toward the high end. This will give you a place to stay warm and get your bearings before making your sleeping area.

If you're setting up permanent shelter to sleep under, construct your lean-to a lot lower to the ground. Once you get everything built, close in the ends of your lean-to with brush and vegetation so the only opening is the front side. The fire should be built in front of this opening in the open air. For this type of fire you need a long coal bed that will generate heat over the length of your body. You can also reflect a lot of the fire's heat toward your sleeping quarters by building a wall out of larger logs behind the fire. Simply drive a couple of sticks in the ground to set the logs against and build your fire in front of them.

In damp or cooler areas, we build "swamp beds" underneath our poncho roof. Swamp beds—raised sleeping platforms fashioned from sticks or saplings—are quick to build. Start by driving four forked sticks in the ground as the support posts. Two longer sticks are placed in the forks, parallel to the ground, and the top is floored with smaller sticks and vegetation. Make the sleeping platform around 24 inches wide and a couple feet off the ground. This system keeps the ground from sucking body heat away from you and also prevents a lot of bugs and other crawling things from bothering you in the night. Another trick to keep bugs at bay is to soak the swamp bed support legs with DEET or other insect repellent.

If you have no poncho or other covering, improvised shelter can be built beside large fallen trees. Placing sticks over the tree in lean-to fashion and covering with smaller sticks and vegetation will protect you from a lot of the elements. If available, large leaves like banana and Bird of Paradise can be fashioned into a leak-proof shingle roof by starting at the bottom of the roof and lapping more leaves on top as you go up. Lean-to shelters built from debris or plants should have a steeper angle than a poncho lean-to in order to make them more waterproof. Also, be careful when selecting dead trees for one side of your shelter—just like you, a lot of animals and other creatures seek shelter in these same locations.

Many trees in tropical forests have large buttresses at their base. These can provide instant shelter by sitting between two buttresses and fashioning a quick roof from palm fronds or other materials. One word of warning when using tall standing trees as shelter: In a thunderstorm you're sitting at the base of a tall lightning rod.

There are many other types of improvised shelters for

Jungle adventurer Barry Masters rests beside his jungle camp
built with the items in his survival kit and a machete.

just about any climate, including snow caves, debris shelters, rock caves, woven-leaf huts, natural depressions, rock
outcroppings, and countless others. Use your common
sense, and always be looking for possible shelter when
trekking through the wilderness, especially before periods
of bad weather or toward the evening hours. Just be sure
you check out an area before deciding to spend a night in
it. There's nothing worse than waking up in a hole beside
that sow grizzly bear you ran from a few hours earlier. Also
weigh your options—is it better to just get a nice fire going

and prop up against a tree for some quick shuteye, or should you take the time to build a structure that you're only going to abandon after a few hours?

WATER

In a true survival situation you would naturally acquire water from any available river or stream. This water could then be purified by boiling in improvised pots or filtering through makeshift filters, or you could just hope for the best and drink it without treatment. But what do you do when running water is not present, or you wish to add an extra layer of protection against human or animal contamination? The best alternative method is extraction of water from plants.

Especially in tropical regions but also in many other places around the world, most of the plant life is soaked to the core with water. Retrieving it is relatively simple once you know what you're looking for. Just remember that water procured from plants should not be stored for more than 24 hours due to the onset of fermentation. Drink it as soon as possible, then procure more.

Live banana trees are excellent producers and generally safe sources of water. Cut the tree down with a knife or machete, leaving a short stump protruding from the ground. Hollow the inside of the stump to produce a bowl shape. After a few hours, the live root system will fill the bowl with water. The first few bowlfuls will have a slightly bitter taste, but they are safe for drinking. After drinking the bowl dry, always place a banana leaf over the bowl to prevent direct evaporation and to protect it from bugs and animals. The stump will continue to produce water for approximately three days.

Although we have used this system during survival education training seminars, the irony of it is that most banana plants are located close to villages, which means a short walk to an easier source of water. Yet the value in telling you about this technique is that there are many other soft-cored trees that will do the same thing. Palm trees, for instance, are abundant in many types of forest and can provide water in this manner.

Another source of fresh water is water vines. Found throughout jungle and tropical regions, they are easily identified by their size and shape (3 to 6 inches in diameter and round, not flat like ribbon vine). Cutting a yard-long piece from a water vine will produce a stream of clear running water immediately. Always cut the vine at the top first, then the bottom. If you do it the other way the remaining vine will suck most of the water up before you get the top cut.

If you have chosen the wrong vine, water will not be free-flowing and the dripping sap will have an extremely bitter taste and/or cloudy appearance. Do not drink this since it can be highly poisonous. The liquid from water vines will have a neutral or fruity taste—not at all repugnant. The ironic part about true water vines is that some of them are poisonous, but the water produced from them is not. For this reason it is best to not allow any cut portion of the vine to make contact with your skin because rashes and allergic reactions can develop.

Many trees are capable of producing water in the same way as the water vine. Most of these will be large trees with exposed root systems, such as the cecropia, and will produce more than a quart of water from a root of roughly 4 inches in diameter and 36 inches long (the smaller the root, the less water stored inside). The great thing about this is that if you only cut one of the roots the tree will continue to live, unlike the vine that dies after cutting a section out. As with cutting a water vine, always make the first cut on the root close to the tree to keep the water from being sucked up into the system.

If you're lucky enough to be in an area abundant with bamboo, then you can take water directly from its sections by chopping a hole and letting the water flow out. Bamboo also makes great improvised pots and shelter.

Author Mike Perrin gets a drink of water from a jungle vine.

Another resourceful place for finding water is inside the leaf systems of plants. Rainwater will gather in the bowl-like shapes of many tropical plants. Certain plants such as orchids always have some amount of water collected within. Be careful when drinking this water because this secret is well-known to all the insects and wildlife of the forest; it's highly recommended that you boil or filter it before consumption.

Finally, if it's raining, you can construct a simple holding container out of a broad leaf. A few of these will produce plenty of water to fill your canteens.

Many survival books and instructors teach the construction and use of solar stills for water procurement in dry places, saying one will produce up to a liter of water a day. In our opinion it's a damn good way to die of dehydration. We've practiced with this method and have gotten only about two good gulps after eight hours of waiting for water to accumulate. However, if you have enough plastic bags and time to spend, they will produce a little bit of water. The process can also be improvised to make salt water drinkable, so maybe it's worth a quick explanation.

To make the still, you need a clear plastic bag, green leaves or other vegetation, and a small rock or weight. Fill the bag about half full with the vegetation and place the rock inside to make a low point in the bag. Close the bag, tie it off securely, and hang it in direct sunlight. The vegetation will soon give up its moisture in the form of condensation. As the moisture condenses on the bag it will run to the low area, where a small hole can be punctured to drain the water off. Be sure to reseal the hole with a cordage tie or tape so water can begin collecting again. Replace the vegetation as water production slows.

That's the easy solar still to build. If you have nothing but time and like to dig, one can also be made below ground. Dig a hole and place the vegetation inside along with a small catch container. Stretch a clear plastic sheet over the top of the hole and seal around the edges with dirt or rocks. Place a rock on top of the plastic directly over the container. This will form a low point for any moisture to run to and drip into the container. Again, as the sun shines through the plastic, it evaporates the moisture from the vegetation. Moisture condenses on the bottom of the plastic and drips into the catch container. If you only have access to salt water, soaking rags or vegetation in the salt water, then extracting the condensation through the still produces drinkable distilled water.

As stated, we do not recommend solar stills of any type as a life-saving water producer. It would take many of these working simultaneously to produce enough water to sustain life in one person. We have tried them, and they do work, but the content produced for the amount of work required is not worth it. It is at best a method for distilling water. Having said that, it is a skill to put in the back of your brain for that time it may be useful.

When you think about it, the possibilities for finding water are endless. Look at it this way: If anything is growing or living nearby, then it typically requires water. If you look hard enough, you can tap into that water source. Even along saltwater beaches you can find fresh water by digging behind the natural sand dunes. Other tricks include looking for tree crotches or crevices in rocks that may contain puddles. Many plant roots can be mashed to release their water content. Birds will usually fly toward water in the evening, and heavily traveled animal trails usually lead to a water source. The Australian aborigines tie tufts of grass to their feet and walk through dew-covered ground. The grass absorbs the moisture and can be distilled or wrung into a container for purification.

FOOD

Most wilderness newcomers want to learn an absolute way to determine the edibility of plants, animals, and fish taken from the wild. There is none. Sure, we could quote you the "edibility test" from the *U.S. Army Survival Field*

Manual, and you might do okay with it, but it is very unsound advice. Using that method could potentially poison someone who would otherwise just go hungry for a few days. Edibility tests, therefore, should only be used as a last resort when it is determined that a survival situation will be long term and you are faced with the choice of eating unfamiliar animal and plant life or dying.

The notion of people becoming stranded or lost in the backcountry for long periods of time is a popular misconception. When you think about it, when was the last time you heard of someone who actually found themselves in such a desperate long-term situation? The last incident I can think of took place in 1992, when a young man named Christopher McCandless decided to live a subsistent existence in the Alaskan bush and ended up dead due to an incredible lack of knowledge of all the edible plants and animals around him. In fact, most people who become lost in a wilderness area are only lost for a brief period of time, and few of them are ever truly "lost" to begin with. They end up losing their bearings in a place they are otherwise familiar with in the sense that they made a decision to be in that locale—they didn't just end up there by accident.

For example, if I get lost in the Amazon Basin, it's because I chose to travel to that region. Regardless of the fact that I may not know my exact location, I do know I am still in a tropical environment, and the plant and animal life is going to be the same throughout that region. I therefore know I can eat the hearts of palm trees, munch on large nutritious grubs found in decaying wood, gather various fruits and nuts that I have eaten in other tropical areas, cook a land turtle into soup in its own shell, and dine on many other foods common to the tropics.

Another misconception that has become a part of survival lore is that if you find yourself in a desperate situation without food, you can eat whatever the animals eat. This advice can get you killed. For example, squirrels in the southeastern part of the United States regularly eat the nuts from a buckeye tree. These are highly poisonous to humans, and about the only use we have for them is to make fish-stunning poison. Monkeys in South America eat fruit from trees that are high in cyanide poison. If humans followed suit they would die quickly.

We could fill the rest of this book with information on what's edible and what's not in the wilderness and still not cover everything. Relying on wild foraging as a way to stay comfortably full of food takes a lot of study and practice with knowledgeable instructors. The secret to survival foods, therefore, is to familiarize yourself with regional foods that have high nutritional value, are easy to recognize, and are safe to eat. If you don't have the time or commitment to do this, at the very least get yourself a color photo guidebook that absolutely identifies a plant, animal, or fish and its edibility.

Two of the better food-gathering methods for most wilderness areas are having the ability to fish and trap small mammals. Of course these skills take practice and a few tools to be successful. Can you make improvised snares, deadfalls, and other traps that actually work? Can you make a primitive hook, line, and sinker from your clothing and what's available in the forest? If you answered "no" to these questions, then make sure you have an appropriately stocked survival kit on your person at all times and practice using it because you may have to fall back on it to feed yourself.

Another secret is to forage only foods that are high in nutritional value and are easily gathered in sufficient quantities; otherwise, it may take more energy to gather the food than its nutritional value will replace. In other words, why would you burn precious calories chasing a wild hog many miles through the woods when there's a lake full of fish in front of you? Similarly, why work to cut down an 18-inch diameter palm tree for its heart when the ground is covered with peach palm fruits?

Our team has traveled for a weeks at a time in tropical jungles and subtropical swamps feeding ourselves with

Butchering a small alligator for food in Central America. In a survival situation, nothing from the animal is wasted. Even the bones are boiled for the nutrition found inside the marrow.

nothing but a machete and what the forest offered. We can comfortably do this because we know the areas we travel to and have studied under some of the best indigenous guides there. However, put our team in the middle of the arctic and we would be challenged to stay fed and warm because we haven't researched or had experience in that type of environment. This is not to say we would die—simply knowing the basics of food gathering for any region gives the survivor a basic knowledge to build on anywhere in the world.

The bottom line is that in most survival situations food is just not that important because the human body can survive many days without proper nourishment. Unless you feel you know you will be facing a long-term survival scenario, don't worry too much about food or having to live off the land. Once you get to your destination, you can learn more in one day from the locals than a book will teach you in weeks of study. So do some basic research on the edible plants and animals in your area of travel, keep a few tools handy, practice with them when you get the chance, and if you are ever in a true survival situation, you probably won't lose any more weight than you need to anyway. There are far greater survival skills to be learned than the ability to gather food.

MAP AND COMPASS NAVIGATION

For anyone who will be traveling the backcountry, where things like marked trails and other luxuries of civilization are nonexistent, learning compass and map skills should be one of your top priorities. Stepping away from the beaten path can easily lead the unprepared adventurer into unfamiliar territory. Couple this disorientation with ensuing panic and the victim often becomes solely dependent on guesswork in a blind attempt to become found. All of this displeasure can be avoided by learning the basic principles and procedures of map and compass work.

Topographic maps are considered a must-have for serious wilderness travel. Their proper use with a compass will help you avoid difficult areas as well as allow you to track distance and rate of travel, but the biggest advantage to this skill is the confidence of always knowing where you are.

Although there are no existing topographic maps for many Third World regions, we are including details for understanding them since this knowledge will help you to understand maps in general. Any map is better than none, but if at all possible, always get your hands on good topographic maps of the area you are visiting. Even if they are not United States Geological Survey (USGS) maps, an international standard for understanding them is typically followed.

Using a compass and map is relatively simple, even for beginners. If you are in a wilderness setting with a map of the region, the first step is to orient the map so it's lying exactly as the land is. To do this, you must have a baseplate compass, also known as an orienteering compass. It has a rectangular base with an arrow clearly marked "bearing" or "direction of travel." Mounted on top of the base is a housing, or dial, holding the floating needle. This dial can be rotated and has the cardinal points (North, South, East, and West, marked as N, S, E, W), along with numerical degree markings that intersect with the bearing arrow as it is rotated. On top of the dial there's another outline of an arrow that is a little larger than the floating needle. For instructional purposes in this book, the arrow on the compass base will be called the "bearing," and the arrow marked on the rotating dial will be referred to as "outlined."

Note that the floating needle is marked on the end that points to north. When the needle is lined up inside of the outlined arrow, it is called "boxing" a compass. Proper boxing always places the needle's north-pointing end inside the tip of the outlined arrow.

At the bottom of a topographic map are two small arrows; one is marked "MN" for magnetic north and the other is marked by a small star at the point representing true north. The difference between magnetic and true north is called "declination" and will vary depending on your position in the world. Every good topographic map will have the declination printed on it. If you do not have topos of the region you plan to travel, check its average declination before you leave home. Depending on the area, declination could be a major factor even for gross navigation.

To orient your topo map for finding location, place the compass on the map and align the bearing arrow with the true north line. Hold the base steady and rotate the compass dial until the outlined arrow is aligned with the magnetic north (MN) line on the map. The whole map is then rotated, being careful not to move the compass, until the floating compass needle is boxed inside the outlined arrow. The map is now oriented to your physical location and ready for use.

Even if you do not have a topo map, the same process can be used with detailed country or area maps. Although they will not show topography or have the declination noted, they will still have prominent features and "North" marked on them. Simply place your compass on the map and rotate the whole map until the compass needle points exactly the same as the "North" arrow marked on the map, then rotate the map further to offset for the average declination you researched before leaving home. Now you will be oriented to true north.

As long as your visibility is good and the map has good detail, you should now be able to do rough triangulation and get a general idea of your location. Triangulation is a fairly simple technique if you are able to get a good view of the surrounding area. The following instructions may seem difficult, but once you practice with a map, compass, and vantage point it becomes pretty easy.

First of all, triangulation is best done from a high point so you can see a wider area of the topography and how it blends together. Look around and find a prominent feature such as a high mountain peak or large lake, then locate it on your map by carefully studying the surrounding areas and comparing the oriented map with actual topography.

Don't jump to rapid conclusions during this process; take your time and look at all details. It is very easy to see a feature on a topo map and immediately assume that it is what you are looking at in the distance. Or you could have the opposite problem: In serious mountainous or canyon country, the jumble of peaks, cliffs, and ridges in front of you may seem impossible to distinguish from one another. You can even get it backward: An abrupt peak on the map can resemble an abrupt valley and fool the untrained topo map reader. Before you place your survival on topographic maps, be sure you understand its symbols and layout, then practice, practice, practice in familiar territory. It's not as difficult as you would imagine, but it can be very intimidating to the untrained, especially when the dread of being lost has entrenched itself in the person's mind.

Once you are sure of the feature's location on the map, mark it with a pencil. Holding the compass in your hand, point the bearing arrow towards the actual feature and rotate the compass dial until the needle is boxed by the outlined arrow. Direction to the feature will be the degree marking that aligns with the bearing arrow on the base.

Without further movement of the dial, set the compass on the oriented map, allowing one of the long edges on the compass base to cross over the feature marked in pencil. Rotate the compass until the floating needle is again boxed inside the outlined arrow, being sure to not move the oriented map and to keep the base edge over the pencil-marked feature. Once this step is complete, draw a line along the edge of the compass that will intersect the pencil-marked feature. Your actual location is somewhere along that line.

Now do this two more times using different identifiable features and drawing a new line for each new bearing. The three lines on the map will intersect to form a small triangular shaped area. If the features have been properly identified and the process followed correctly, your location will be within that area. (Note: Because most compass bases are small, line extension may be necessary to form the intersection. This can be done by folding the map over and using one of its straight edges as a guide.)

But what if you find yourself in dense vegetation or low areas, making it difficult to locate prominent features for triangulation? You can overcome this by evaluating your map and traveling a bearing until you're in a better location for precise pinpointing. But how do you do this? Orient the map and compare it to what the actual topogra-

Special Forces Engineer Mike Benish takes a compass
reading during a hike up a Central American river.

phy looks like. For example, how does the river flow
around the hillside? Does it make a complete horseshoe
shape or just a 90 degree bend? Determine this and then
look for a similar feature on the map. If there's more than
one such feature on the map, then look around for a second landmark that may corroborate which bend in the
river on the map is the one you can see in front of you. In
a worst-case scenario, such as a totally flat primary jungle,
then the only option is to walk a straight bearing until
some unique feature presents itself.

Again, this should never be done in a hurried manner.

Always take the time to study your surroundings and map carefully. By doing so, you should be able to get a reasonable idea of your location.

After marking your believed location in pencil, find your target destination on the map. Now place the center of the compass directly over the area where you believe you are located. Point the bearing arrow toward the target area on the map and rotate the compass dial until the needle is boxed. You now have a bearing in degrees to your target location.

To walk a bearing, place the compass in your hand with the bearing arrow pointing directly in front of you and rotate your body (not the compass or dial) until the needle is boxed. This will be the direction of travel to your target. Make a note of this bearing (degree number) for future reference and to adjust your compass dial if it accidentally gets moved.

You can travel along this bearing by locating an object some distance directly ahead of you and walking to it. Once you reach the object, find another on the same bearing and move to it. This process will keep you walking a straight line toward your destination. If there is no object to orient on and you are traveling with a companion, have him become your target by walking a ways in front of you and moving until he lines up with your bearing. You then walk to him and repeat the process.

Many times one bearing may not allow you to reach your destination due to obstacles such as large lakes or sheer cliffs. If you must change bearings for easier mobility, then be sure to denote every change for backtracking purposes. For example, if you are walking a bearing of 90 degrees and must turn 30 degrees toward the south to avoid an obstacle, then mark your original bearing (90 degrees) and your new bearing (which will be 120 degrees) on a piece of paper with pencil. You will need this information to backtrack accurately if the need arises. Should you begin to retrace your steps, you must add or subtract 180 degrees to the bearings on the paper. If the original bearing you had marked is less than 180 degrees, then add 180 degrees to this number for your reverse bearing. If the original bearing marking is more than 180 degrees, then subtract 180 from the original number to get your reverse bearing.

We also suggest using Ranger beads or some other pace-counting device in conjunction with a map and compass. Ranger beads will give you a pretty accurate accounting of distance traveled. If you don't have Ranger beads, use small pebbles. Place a handful in your right trouser pocket and every 65 full paces (one pace = every time your left foot hits the ground), move a pebble from the right pocket to the left. If you ever need to know how far you have traveled, then count the pebbles in the left pocket. Each pebble will represent roughly 100 meters (or a little over 100 yards) for an average adult.

All of this may sound complicated, but once the process is applied and practiced a few times, it becomes simple. If you choose not to practice, then keep this book as an instruction guide in your survival kit. If you can't fit the whole book, photocopy this section only and store it in a zip-lock plastic bag with your other navigation aids in your kit.

If you go into a wilderness area with only a compass and no map, then always know which cardinal point (N, S, E, W) intersects a river, main highway, or other form of civilization in relation to the area you are traveling in. In other words, if you know a north-south road is somewhere to the east of your location, then boxing your compass and walking in the direction of the E will bring you to it. When using a compass for this purpose, declination plays less of a role since all you need to do is walk a straight line in the general direction of civilization. Although this may not be the shortest or easiest route, it's better than walking in circles or getting yourself deeper into trouble.

There are many primitive techniques for determining gross direction if you have no compass. Most of these work by using the sun since it always rises in the east and sets in the west. Although we are not going to detail all of them here, a simple one to use is the shadow stick. This works by a driving a stick about 18 inches tall into a sunny area of the ground. The sun will cast a shadow of the stick. At the end of that shadow place a marker on the ground such as a small stone. The rotation of the Earth will cause the shadow to slowly change positions. Wait about 30 minutes and place another marker at the end of the moved shadow. Draw a line between your two marks. Toe the line with your left foot closest to the first marked position. You are now facing north.

Some survival instructors will warn you that a shadow stick will not work below the equator. Once again this is pure bullshit. Regardless of where you are in the world, the sun always rises in the east and sets in the west, so the shadow stick method works the same in Argentina as it does in Alabama. The only exception to this is at higher latitudes approaching the Earth's poles. It doesn't work as well once you go more than 20 degrees from the equator since the sun is lower on the horizon, making it difficult to pinpoint the long shadows and east/west movement of the sun.

SIGNALING

It is truly amazing how fast you can get lost in unknown heavy wilderness. For this reason, never take off without a compass and signal device in your possession.

Basic distress signaling is quick to learn and will save your butt in a jam. Fires, smoke, mirrors, flares, battery-operated strobes, and ground markings are all excellent means of long-distance signaling. For shorter ranges, rescue whistles, flashlights, and reflective tape will work.

If you're stuck in the wilderness with no other signaling device, three fires can be used (three being the universal sign for distress), but you must maintain them in a constant state of readiness. Waiting until you hear a plane before building your fires is useless. By the time you get the kindling burning good, the aircraft will probably already be landing at its destination. The only exception I could imagine to this would be if you had several gallons of flammable fluid or large piles of bone-dry flash tinder available. The average adventurer is not going to be that lucky, so if fire is your only means to signal a rescuer, then get ready for a lot of work.

First of all, find or make a large clearing free of obstructions, heavy overgrowth, or forest canopy. In dense forest the suggested size is a minimum of 60 square yards (50 square meters) to provide an aircraft with a wider field of view. Next you need to gather an abundance of fire-making materials, then build three small fires equally spaced in a straight line or triangle. Separate them a minimum of 50 feet apart if possible, but make sure they're close to being equally spaced. Be sure to gather enough wood to maintain a decent sized campfire in each of them at all times. Also gather green vegetation such as grasses, treetops with leaves, or other broad leaf plant material.

If you hear a plane at night, quickly build up all three fires with small pieces of dry wood or dead leaves to produce as much light and flame as possible. If the plane is passing by in daylight, then cover the fires with the green vegetation to produce heavy smoke, grab some type of signaling device, such as a white T-shirt, and wave it frantically. If a search and rescue plane locates you, the pilot will usually do at least one direct flyover at low altitude. If he "waves" at you with his wings, that's the international sign of acknowledging you are there and needing assistance.

You can also make ground signals from logs, ponchos, or anything else that is visible from the air. Use the following international codes to communicate your needs. A straight line means you need immediate evacuation or medical assistance. An F indicates a need for food or water. X means you are unable to move. An arrow communicates your direction of travel if you plan on moving from that location. A triangle represents a safe landing zone for rescue aircraft. LL means everything is okay and no assistance is needed. These are just some of the international signals, but they should be all that is ever required for most survival scenarios.

If the plane is close enough, you can flick your flashlight on and off to signal the international distress Morse code of SOS (three shorts, three longs, three shorts). Pocket signal strobes are also good for nighttime signaling. The units are very compact, battery operated, and can be switched on and off to conserve battery power. Another all-purpose distress signal device we have used when working with the Peruvian military's downed pilot survival school is light, compact pen flares. A pilot's survival kit will usually contain three such flares that will launch a bright red light more than 200 feet into the sky. These are not fireworks to impress the native population. If you're in the wilderness with these or any other signaling device, use them only in an emergency.

For daytime signaling of aircraft, nothing beats a signal mirror. The better the mirror, the better the chances of you being seen. We suggest the U.S. Air Force type because it has a unique aiming screen that is very accurate for flashing a pilot's eye many miles away.

If you have no signal mirror, then find anything with high reflectivity in sunlight and poke a hole in its center so you can see through it. To aim it, extend an arm in front of you, hold up two fingers in a peace sign configuration, and box the aircraft inside these fingers. With your other hand, move the reflective object up to your eye and peer through the hole, finding the aircraft between your two fingers. While keeping your eye on the plane, move the signaling device around until you see a flash of light cross over your peace sign. You have just flashed the aircraft.

Do not hold the signal static on the plane; flash it back and forth instead. The reason for this is because pilots see numerous reflective objects when flying, so unless they are flashing at regular intervals it does not raise a concern. Once you receive a positive signal from the plane that you have been seen, quit signaling so it does not confuse the situation.

For marking your camp in the middle of a forest or on a riverbank, carry pieces of reflective tape. If you wander off from camp or go down river for the night, this makes it extremely easy to find your way back. Simply wrap a piece of tape around a tree at the camp or on the bank and use your flashlight to locate it on the return trip. This also works as a rescue marker to attract the lights of anyone searching for a lost adventurer.

SELF-RESCUE

If you find yourself lost and decide to self-rescue, use the instructions in the navigation section above to keep yourself moving in the right direction. If you have done your pre-trip homework properly, you should have a rough idea in which cardinal direction you'll find civilization.

If you're totally lost and confused, always remember that water almost always runs toward civilization. Following streams will eventually lead to larger bodies of water. Larger bodies of water will eventually lead to humans. If you're not sure where to find flowing water, then look for animal trails since they typically lead toward fresh water supplies. You can also watch the direction birds are flying early in the evening hours; they will probably be heading toward water.

This technique actually saved one of our past clients. After returning home from one of our jungle survival expeditions, he decided to take another adventure into the jungles of Belize. After becoming disoriented and lost for most of the day, he remembered our instruction about following water. He took a chance and started following a river downstream. The next day he walked into a small village along the riverbank—tired and hungry, but safe.

In heavy forest it is very easy to become disoriented once you move outside the visual range of your camp or trail. If you're traveling with companions, don't be ashamed to shout or blow a few bursts into your rescue whistle in order to get a response and regain your sense of direction. If you must wander off from camp, take a quick compass reading of your direction so you can backtrack if necessary. If you are traveling by trail, road, or river, make a mental note of its direction so you can easily walk a compass bearing that intersects it if you become disoriented.

Another technique we use to find our way back to camp is hacking a back trail as we move through the forest. Every so often, cut a visible sign on the back sides of trees with your machete or knife. Once you start back, the hack signs will be visible. This can also be done by breaking small plants so they will be visible on your return trip. If you use this technique, always break the plant so the underside of the leaf will be visible on your return, as this side will contrast better against the forest than the top side and will be notably out of place when you're looking for sign.

WATERBORNE SURVIVAL

During one of our adventures in Central America, we participated in a survival course setup for a major television series. Parts of the course involved river crossings and white-water rafting. These events took place far away from civilization, and it was probably one of the more dangerous trips we have worked on.

A couple years after our work there, a close friend of ours was involved in a white-water rafting accident on one of the same rivers. One team member drowned and our friend nearly died when their raft capsized after attempting to run the river at flood stage. When the boat went belly up, everyone lost what survival gear they had, leaving them barefooted in shorts many miles from any town or village. The surviving team members hiked through several miles of jungle to notify rescue personnel, and the victim's body was eventually recovered.

The point is, water adventures of any type are extremely dangerous and should never be taken for granted. Even if part of your Third World travel consists of lazily boating up a calm river to view the bird and wildlife activity, always have some type of personal flotation device (PFD) with you. If there are no commercially manufactured PFDs available, then improvise one by inflating a water bladder or trapping some air in waterproof gear bags. Another trick is to wrap and seal a backpack in a poncho by sealing the opening with a cord and floating the gear with the tied part upright. If you have two ponchos, wrap one over the pack and tie it, then do the same to the other poncho but position its tied side exactly opposite from the first one's.

During all of our expeditions, we carry digital video cameras and 35mm still cameras with various lenses to record our work. All of this is stored in a large Dry-Seal bag. Once we're on the boat, we open the bag, allowing air to be trapped inside with the camera gear. Then we reseal for an instant PFD while keeping our gear dry.

Other life-saving tips for river travel include never having your pack attached to you while standing, boarding, riding, or operating anywhere near a boat. If you fall overboard in deep water, you're more than likely going to drown as you sink like a rock. Travel with light clothes on the river for the same reason. If you get cool, drape a poncho over yourself. Whatever you do, keep your emergency survival kit, papers, and cash inside a waterproof bag that will float and keep it beside you at all times.

If you do get stranded in deep wilderness and have to use the river system to escape, you may want to build a quick raft to float you and your gear out. In jungle environments this is often a much better option than trying to walk out; during the wet season it may be required after a couple days of rain. In fact, if you ever find yourself in the tropical lowlands and the rains start, do your best impression of Noah and start building a floating platform right away.

A simple raft can be constructed from bamboo (or any wood that has good buoyancy) lashed together with vines, rope, or cordage. It does not have to be a monstrous ocean-going vessel; all you need is something that will support your weight and allow you to drift downstream. In fact the bigger you make it the harder it will be to handle through log jams and river bends. Do not attempt primitive raft travel in serious white water, and never attempt to swim your way to safety. Even in the tropics, wilderness streams and rivers are extremely cool, and hypothermia will catch up to you. Try to stay as dry and as mobile as possible when moving down rivers or through flooded wetlands.

Rafts have been literal life savers for us on a couple of expeditions during the wet season in South America. On one trip we were many miles back in the heart of the low jungle along the Brazil/Peru border when it rained nonstop for two days. After it was over, there wasn't a dry piece of land to be found because the water rose more than six feet. We managed to raft our way out of the swamp back to the main river and our base boat.

Another good aspect to raft travel is the ability to cover a lot of distance with minimal work. The river does the paddling for you; all you really need is a long pole to keep the raft pushed away from trouble spots. Rafting also keeps you safe from a lot of the jungle's critters such as ants and other bugs that like to take up residence on your body, especially during floods.

Once the raft is waterborne, the only serious complication you will likely encounter is getting it around or over logjams and other debris. You will be able to hack through most of these with a machete, but if it's a major obstruction you may have to go over it. This is harder than it sounds but not impossible. First, hack a place in the obstructing log; then peel the bark from another tree (such as a cecropia) and place the slick inner side (cambium) of that bark on the hacked areas. You now literally have a greased runway to shove the raft over.

Randall's Adventure & Training clients use a makeshift raft to navigate themselves out of the inner depths of the jungle.

Raft travel also allows you to travel at night since you're basically on a superhighway in the wilderness. You would think that getting lost would be a minor concern when rafting down small tributaries that flow directly to a main river system. This is far from the truth, especially if the area you are traveling through is flooded or swampy. In order to stay on course under darkness, you have to watch for the right signs as you move downstream. Use your flashlight only to judge distance to the shore because white light on water produces a lot of confusing shadows and night blindness. To

Nothing is more important than practicing your wilderness survival skills. Here a group of adventure travelers practice rope skills being taught by a military officer.

keep yourself in the channel of the watercourse, look toward the night sky and follow the open areas void of canopy and trees. Never follow any rapid water flow in flooded areas; these are usually false channels that are nothing more than excess river water draining into low-lands. Finally, watch for certain types of vegetation that only flourish in the rivers. Finding thick patches of water lettuce, hyacinth, and other water plants is a good sign that you are on the main river.

Traveling in wilderness waterways and lowlands is serious business. You have to stay alert, avoid hypothermia, and work slowly to keep dangers at bay. It's very easy to let your mind wander and suddenly become dragged into the murky depths by a snag or step into a hole deeper than you are tall with your pack on your back. Just because the water appears calm doesn't mean it's not deadly. Undertow, sunken logs, rocks, vines, and many other dangers have the potential to kill you. Be careful and use common sense when operating in and around water in wilderness areas.

As we stated in the beginning of this chapter, there are plenty of books, videos, and instructors on wilderness survival. In this chapter we've only touched on a few techniques that have been useful to us during our travels in Third World tropics, jungles, and wilderness areas around the world. We refuse to make the claim that our way is the only way, but know that what you have read here comes from actual hands-on experience. Hopefully these skills may come in handy to some future adventurer faced with a life-threatening experience, but before going bush we recommend that all travelers study, acquire experience, and practice with a reputable instructor.

CHAPTER 10

Wilderness First Aid

During our survival training classes and expeditions around the world, we always have someone on board who is trained in emergency care just in case the worst happens many miles from a hospital. If you don't have the luxury of being accompanied by a trained professional, at least get a minimal amount of training in emergency first aid before your departure. Even the most basic understanding of emergency care can save you or others a lot of misery and possibly even your life. As with every other aspect of adventure travel, preparation is the key to success.

ISSUES SURROUNDING WILDERNESS FIRST AID

Before we delve into specific treatments for injuries and ailments common to adventure travel, let's look at a few simple ways to prevent serious medical problems from arising.

- Always travel with a companion and let others know where you're going and how long you intend to be gone.
- Always have a prearranged evacuation route and meeting points.
- Avoid using drugs or alcohol while in the backcountry.
- Always carry adequate food and water or at least have safe ways to purify local water.
- Anticipate weather changes and carry extra dry clothing.
- Learn basic navigation and have good maps of the area.
- Have an extra pair of eyeglasses in your kit if you are dependent on glasses or contact lenses.
- Always ask if your partner or traveling companions have special medical conditions such as allergies to specific medications, food, or insects, and if anyone has ever had a heat-related illness.
- Never approach or provoke wild animals, because "playing" with the animals can cost you your life.

A good example of this final rule occurred during one of our overseas expeditions. A local, who had hand-caught hundreds of alligators in the past, made a simple mistake and received a nasty bite. Swelling and pain due to infection ensued, and without proper first-aid treatment, antibiotics, and a quick evacuation, he could have lost his hand or even his life.

There are many medical problems that can occur in remote areas. Due to length restrictions, we have directed our attention to the most probable occurrences for back-country travelers. The treatments described are general overviews only and should not be considered as final instruction in first aid. Anyone wishing to learn proper first aid should do so through a reputable instructor.

HYPOTHERMIA

As we noted earlier in the book, hypothermia—or the abnormal lowering of body temperature—is one of the most dangerous medical emergencies you may face while adventure traveling. Hypothermia can strike even in wet tropical regions, so it is imperative that you learn to recognize its initial symptoms (including a glazed expression, fatigue, confusion, clumsiness, uncontrolled shivering, and the victim's refusal to recognize the problem and help himself) and act quickly to get the victim's core body temperature back to normal as fast as possible.

Nothing will put heat back into a wet body quicker than removing all wet clothing and drying off. We always keep an emergency pair of clothes sealed away in a waterproof bag for these situations. If you only have a dry space blanket, consider the option of shedding all the wet clothes, wrapping up tightly in the blanket, and sitting near a fire or other heat source. If you have a companion—male or female—and hypothermia is setting in, then both of you should remove all wet clothing and find anything dry to wrap up in together. Keep your heads covered, and embrace each other until you regain body heat.

Here's a trick we have used if you're extremely cold and the fire you built doesn't seem to warm you well enough. Once the fire burns down to good coals, scrape a few of them off to one side, put your poncho on, and then squat down directly over the coals so the poncho bottom seals against the ground. This will keep all the heat inside the poncho and around your body. You can also heat rocks in the fire, move them out to the side, and squat down over them for the same effect. (Just be careful to never use river rocks in a fire—the trapped moisture inside them will turn to steam and can cause a pretty good explosion when it rips the rock apart.) The only drawback to this wilderness central heating system is that you have to be careful not to get burned, especially so if you've stripped off your wet clothing before doing it. Typically it's nothing more than burning your ass from squatting too low, but if you're not paying attention, your poncho may start smoldering or your clothes may catch on fire—but at least you'll be warm!

HEAT-RELATED ILLNESS

One of the most frequent medical situations experienced in the wilderness is heat-related illness, which includes heat cramps, heat exhaustion, and heat stroke. These illnesses are caused from dehydration and loss of electrolytes through sweating and inadequate intake of calories from food. It is important to know if any of your travel companions have suffered a heat-related illness in the past because they will be more susceptible to recurrences.

The symptoms for heat exhaustion include cool, pale, and clammy skin, weakness, headache, nausea, dizziness, thirst, rapid pulse, chills, slightly raised body temperature, and low blood pressure. Treatment should include immediate rest in a cool area, removal of excess clothing, giving fluids to drink, and wetting the body with cool water. If there is not an abundance of water available, remember that water is better "in you than on you." For severe cases, add a quarter teaspoon of salt and six teaspoons of sugar to a quart of water and have the patient drink in regular intervals. The bush equivalent to prepackaged oral rehydration salts, this technique of electrolyte replacement should only be done sparingly. The best way to replace sodium is through food.

Heat stroke is a serious medical emergency that can kill in a matter of minutes. The symptoms are basically the same as heat exhaustion except the body's core temperature can exceed 106 degrees. The victim frequently displays severe personality changes and a lowered level of consciousness. The skin will be hot and can either be sweaty or dry. The mental status of the victim will decline, usually manifested by slurred speech and loss of motor skills, eventually leading to coma. Immediately suspect heat stroke in any person who suddenly collapses when in a hot environment.

First aid must be rendered immediately because this is an absolute medical emergency. The secret to treating heat stroke is cooling the body immediately and evacuating the patient as soon as possible. Remove all of the victim's clothing, spray his entire body with water, and fan him vigorously, which will release heat through convection and evaporation. Immerse the victim in ice water if possible, or place ice packs on the back of his neck and on his armpits, lower back, and groin. Be sure to monitor the patient's core temperature, and stop the cooling process once his temperature reaches 100 degrees or else the body can have a reverse reaction and become severely hypothermic.

LACERATIONS AND BLEEDING

Cuts and lacerations are common in the wilderness. The small bleeders are usually easy to control by direct pressure and can be protected against dirt and debris with such dressings as Band-Aids, sterile gauze pads, sterile strips, or by taping the wound closed. You should rarely attempt to sew a wound closed, especially when it cannot be irrigated properly, because debris can be trapped inside and, with decreased drainage, can cause severe infections.

Serious bleeding should be controlled via direct pressure and pressure dressings. If the bleeding is from an extremity, elevate the injured area above heart level while continuing to apply direct pressure. (Two situations when you would not use elevation would be fractures and envenomization.) Another method for decreasing hemorrhage is to apply pressure to points on the joint above the injury where arteries run over bones close to the skin (called "indirect pressure").

Although most wounds can and should be closed with pressure and dressings, there are a few times when sewing or stapling is an asset, such as clean head or face wounds where it is difficult to stop the bleeding. If a wound needs to be closed in this fashion, we suggest thoroughly cleaning the interior of the wound first, then numbing it with subcutaneous injections of 1% lidocaine at intervals around the wound area. After the area is sufficiently numb, pinch the wound closed with hemostats while raising it slightly, then staple or sew as needed. Again, be very careful about closing wounds that have not been cleaned properly. Depending on the wound's location and severity, a drain may need to be inserted before tight closure.

Tourniquets should be used only when arterial or severe venous bleeding cannot be controlled by any other means and the choice is life or limb. Proper procedures for applying a tourniquet should be learned before attempting to save a life with one. If a tourniquet is applied to an accident victim, *always* mark the victim's forehead with the letter T and the date and time the tourniquet was applied. This is done so primary care personnel will immediately know a tourniquet has been put on the patient and can evaluate whether the limb may be saved.

FRACTURES

Broken bones are common backcountry accidents, especially when hiking through tough terrain or navigating over deadfall. Treating fractures can be as simple as applying a splint or as complicated as setting up traction for femur breaks and attempting to control internal bleeding.

When analyzing a patient for broken bones, look for visual misalignment along the bone and pain or loss of motor skills in the affected limb. All jewelry and clothing surrounding the fracture site should be removed due to swelling and for inspection of further damage and bleeding. All associated bleeding must also be controlled.

Simple splints can be made from sticks and rags. A properly splinted extremity must have the joint above and below the fracture site immobilized; the idea is to keep the injured part from moving and creating further damage. Any breakage in the skin should be covered with sterile gauze and

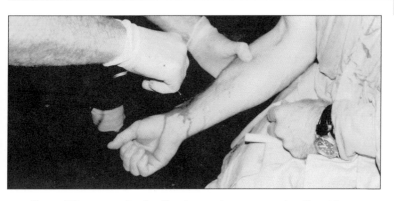

Special Forces medic Jay Stanka tends to a wound suffered by a Randall's Adventure & Training client during a wilderness outing overseas.

tape or with pressure bandages if required. Compound fractures that protrude from the skin should not be reset in a wilderness environment because internal laceration to the arteries from sharp bone fragments is a risk, as is infection from foreign debris entering the area.

Due to the large muscle mass of the thighs, femur fractures are generally the only ones that require traction. Even though you may be far from a hospital, traction should be applied if possible because internal hemorrhaging and severe muscle spasms are frequently associated with these serious injuries. Once traction is set, it should never be released until the victim is in the hands of a primary care facility. Direct and indirect pressure should be used in an attempt to control any bleeding.

DIARRHEA

Diarrhea is another common medical condition for travelers to the Third World. Simple diarrhea can be caused from diet changes, stress, or nervous anticipation associated with new adventures. The more severe forms can be the result of intestinal infections (bacterial, viral, or parasitic), food poisoning, or allergies.

Simple diarrhea will usually take care of itself, but prolonged diarrhea can be serious and cause dehydration due to loss of fluids and electrolytes. The serious cases may be accompanied by lower abdominal cramping, fever, lack of bowel control, and signs of dehydration. Also, others in your group may show signs of having the same condition.

Treatment consists of drinking copious amounts of clear fluids and a gradual return to a normal diet. Steer clear of milk products and meats for at least 48 hours after the diarrhea has stopped, and avoid caffeine and nicotine because they stimulate the intestine and increase dehydration. Pepto-Bismol and Imodium AD should be included in every first-aid bag for simple diarrhea. One of the best treatments is oral rehydration salts, which are usually found in good travel first-aid kits, or you can make the bush equivalent detailed under heat-related illnesses.

INSECT BITES AND STINGS

Insect stings and bites are hard to avoid entirely when in serious bush. Mosquitoes, chiggers, flies, and a whole host of other creatures love to feast on human flesh. For the most part they're relatively harmless except for those that carry disease. The biggest medical problem usually associated with bites is infection due to scratching with dirty fingernails.

Treatment for minor bites and stings is a simple application of Sting-Eze or other product designed to neutralize the venom and remove the discomfort. More serious bites such as those from wasps and spiders can be treated immediately with a Sawyers Extractor followed by close patient monitoring for further signs of envenomization and/or allergic reactions that can produce anaphylactic shock in those who are hypersensitive to the venom. Oral Benadryl will help to keep down mild allergic reactions but will make the person drowsy, and heavy doses can increase the risk of heat-related illness by raising the body's heat output and decreasing sweating.

Some serious bites like those from brown recluse and black widow spiders may not produce pain at the time of the initial bite, although in most all cases pain becomes evident shortly thereafter. Treatment should consist of washing the bite with soap and water, relieving pain with ice packs on the bite, checking the victim's ABCs (airway, breathing, circulation) regularly, and evacuating the victim to a primary care facility. Don't worry—most insect bites are not fatal if allergic reactions are not present.

The best treatment for insect bites is prevention. DEET is a good insect repellent, but care should be taken when applying high concentrations directly to the skin, especially with children, because DEET has been known to cause allergic reactions and can actually be a toxic substance if used in concentrated amounts for a prolonged time. Another good preventive measure is applying permethrin to clothing, although it has caused allergic reactions in some people. When traveling in tropical and other mosquito-infested areas, always use mosquito netting when camping, and apply DEET around your pant legs and boots to keep down chiggers when walking through grassy areas.

ANAPHYLACTIC SHOCK

Anaphylactic shock is a severe allergic reaction in people who are hypersensitive to insect stings, drugs, or even some types of food. It is a serious medical emergency and can cause death rapidly. The majority of deaths are caused by swollen air passages literally suffocating the victim. Due to the dangers of anaphylactic shock, always inquire about your traveling companions' allergies before traveling with them, and be sure you have proper first-aid supplies to deal with any they may have.

Some of the symptoms of anaphylactic shock may include severe itching, shortness of breath, coughing, sneezing, swelling of the throat, chest tightness, convulsions, and vomiting. These usually occur shortly after the victim has been exposed to the agent that caused the allergic reaction.

The seriousness of this problem cannot be stressed enough. If anaphylactic shock occurs, every second counts. The only life-saving treatment is an epinephrine injection, which is why every remote adventure should include a bee sting kit, which includes epinephrine predosed in a syringe with needle. The injection is usually given as an intramuscular shot in the upper arm or thigh. If this is not available, use an asthma inhaler or decongestant spray, and administer antihistamine or decongestant medication. Monitor the patient's ABCs, with special attention to the airway. Keeping the conscious victim sitting in an upright position may also help breathing. First aid for seizures may be necessary. Evacuate as quickly as possible.

SNAKE BITES

The biggest fear among many wilderness travelers is snake bites. Perhaps much of this is due to the myth and incorrect information that surrounds the dangers of venomous snakes and the treatment of bites. As a victim of a copperhead bite, I can say that being bitten by a poisonous snake is painful but nowhere near as serious a medical emergency as anaphylactic shock, heat stroke, heart attack, or other medical situations that can occur with wilderness travelers.

First of all, a high percentage of bites from venomous species are not "hot" (i.e., bites that inject maximum amounts of venom). However, any bite from such snakes should be treated as potential envenomizations, with the victim being evacuated to a proper health care facility. Even with hot bites, you are not going to die in five minutes—calm, steady first-aid treatment and evacuation will serve the victim much better than running or panicking, which increases heart rate and blood flow and creates more stress in the patient.

Let's address some of the myths up front. Under no circumstances should you apply a tourniquet or make incisions into a bite in an attempt to extract venom. Electric shock treatment only hurts the patient and increases heart rate and blood flow. Cold packs or ice should not be used because they do not inactivate the venom. Do not give aspirin because it can cause greater intestinal bleeding and thin the blood. Alcohol should be avoided because it also thins the blood and dilates vessels, causing pooling of blood. Do not attempt to catch or kill the snake due to the possibility of creating another victim and because in many cases antivenin may not be given at the hospital, so snake identification is not a top priority.

If you can locate the bite mark (it may not be readily visible, as noted in the photo), the Sawyers Extractor can be an effective treatment if applied within two or three minutes of the bite. Within this time frame, up to 30 percent of the injected venom can be removed; at 30 minutes up to 3 percent can be. If the extractor is not available within this period of time, don't waste time looking for it; just begin your first-aid procedures.

Keep the victim calm and quiet, since activity and increased heart rate spread the venom quickly through the body. Monitor ABCs (airway, breathing, circulation, in that order) and treat accordingly. Use a sling to immobilize the bitten limb loosely, and keep it at or below heart level. Watch the patient closely for signs of shock or severely lethargic behavior. If antivenin is administered in the field, monitor the patient closely for severe allergic reactions. We suggest that antivenin be used only by trained professionals because the "cure" could actually be worse than the disease since many people are highly allergic to the horse serum used to produce antivenin. Most important, reassure the victim and make all attempts to keep him calm. Although he may be swollen and in serious pain, in most cases a victim of a hot snake bite will not become critical for several hours. In fact, the wound and resulting infection will very likely become more of a threat than the initial bite.

I have treated snake bites on myself and on a family dog and also assisted during treatment of a young girl bitten by a water moccasin. I have learned that in most cases, a poisonous snake bite is not the medical emergency that Hollywood and many others will have you believe. Both animal and human bodies have an amazing resilience to venom and will absorb quite a bit before shutting down. This is one of the main reasons why you should not apply a tourniquet. If you localize the venom with a tourniquet, it prevents the body from slowly absorbing it and produces massive damage at the wound site, sometimes requiring amputation if the bite is on a limb.

We witnessed the results of a tourniquet treatment during one of our trips to Central America. A local had been bitten on the hand by a fer-de-lance and a tourniquet was applied to the arm just above the bite mark. Three weeks later, the hand had become black, the flesh had rotted away, all movement of the hand and fingers had ceased, and the doctors were expecting to amputate to save the man's life.

On the two cases that I personally treated (myself and the dog), the patient was kept calm and well hydrated with a mixture of half Gatorade and half water. (It should be noted here that the sugars and electrolytes in Gatorade are valuable assets for hydration but should never be given full strength during any medical emergency because they will actually use up existing body water while the patient's system attempts to process the Gatorade.) The remainder of my home-remedy snake bite treatment consisted of administering Benadryl to reduce swelling and a regiment of anti-inflammatory steroids.

Of all the first-aid procedures for snake bite, keeping

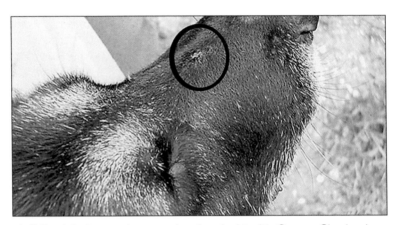

Jeff Randall witnessed a copperhead snake bite his German Shepherd on top of the nose. This photo was taken shortly after the bite. Note the lack of swelling at the bite location and the lack of serious appearance to the wound. The swelling actually occured on the dog's neck, becoming a double-fist-sized watery knot within two hours of the bite. Lesson: depending on the bite location, swelling may localize itself in another area, deceiving those looking for bite marks.

the victim calm is the one absolute must in the survival process. I can't stress this point enough. If you can't remember any other procedure, remember three words: calm, evacuate, and hydrate if possible. Also be aware that small children, the sick, and the elderly have a higher risk of death due to envenomation.

Our experience has been gained from dealing with venomous snakes of the Americas and may not be the right advice for some of the species in Africa, Australia, and other regions. I'm sure some people will disagree with our methods, but the information contained in this section comes from direct experience as both a victim and a primary caretaker for those who suffered venomous bites. All of them are still alive and well as of this writing.

DENTAL PAIN

Dental pain is one of the worst things that can happen to a remote traveler. It can absolutely ruin an otherwise good time. If your trip is going to be for an extended period, we highly recommend visiting a dentist before you leave to make sure no surprise tooth pain comes your way.

The procedures you are about to read are presented for information purposes only and are best performed only by qualified personnel. If you are forced by circumstances to attempt any of these procedures, be sure you have access to epinephrine just in case there is an allergic reaction to the lidocaine.

If you have to deaden an upper tooth, a lidocaine injection should be applied at the base of the tooth's root. A rough scale for determining the injection spot is one and a half times the tooth's length above the gum line. The injection should go into the gum starting from the outside of the mouth. Using a small needle, slowly insert approximately 1 cc of 1% lidocaine.

For lower-jaw teeth, the deadening has to be done via a nerve block. This is a little more tricky than deadening upper-jaw teeth but not impossible. Using your off hand, grasp the victim's mouth by placing your thumb in the corner of the mouth and the rest of your hand around the jaw-bone under the ear. Pinch together and insert the needle in a path that crosses over the opposite side bicuspid to the near side wisdom tooth (the side you have pinched that needs numbing). This will line your needle up. The injection is then made just above the wisdom tooth in the fleshy part of the jaw. Insert your needle about 1 inch deep and slowly inject 1.5 cc of lidocaine. Be sure your injection stays to the inside of the jawbone because if it goes to the outside, it will cause temporary facial paralysis.

TRAVEL FIRST-AID KITS

Massive medical kits are not required to perform basic first aid. The size of your kit will be dependent on the size of your travel group. Naturally if you are traveling solo, your kit has to be able to handle most problems that can arise. However, if you are traveling with a group, the kit can be divided up among the members to make traveling easier. Even when traveling with a group, everyone should have on their person basic first-aid supplies and all personal medications.

We suggest buying a commercial travel kit from a reputable company, then modifying it for the specific needs of your trip. A good store-bought kit will have the basic items and a quick-reference first-aid guide already built in. It is a good idea to separate your enhanced kit into components, such as wound care, eye care, meds, and so forth.

Our expedition kit is housed inside a bright orange waterproof Pelican case and includes basic first-aid items along with the following upgrades. All of these items have been used in one form or another throughout our travels in the Third World. Although our kit is fairly extensive, we list its contents here to give you an idea of the possible scenarios that could be handled in a remote travel emergency with the right gear.

Emergency dental kit. An emergency dental kit can be purchased from reputable first-aid supply houses and will take care of most dental emergencies in the field, including replacing lost fillings and crowns and supplying temporary pain relief for toothaches. We also carry prescription lidocaine along with small needle/syringes just in case we are forced to deaden a tooth in a remote location.

3M disposable skin stapler and staple remover. These staplers are handy tools for closing a wound. They are simpler than sewing, and most folks can handle the pain associated with the quick action of a stapler more so than a drawn-out sewing procedure.

Povidone iodine solution concentrate 10%. This is our preferred wound-cleaning solution. The 3/4-ounce concentrate packages are easy to carry and readily mix with a liter (1 quart) of water to provide the right solution to clean and disinfect dirty wounds before closure. This concentrated packaging takes up less room in your aid kit than the mixed solution commonly found in drugstores.

EpiPen. This is an epinephrine auto-injector. It delivers a 0.3 mg intramuscular dose of epinephrine by simply uncapping and stabbing it into a muscular part of the body. Acquired through a doctor's prescription only, it is still considered a high-priority kit item when traveling in remote areas with a group of people because epinephrine is the only cure for serious anaphylactic shock.

SAM splint. A unique device made from a piece of padded aluminum sheet metal, a SAM splint can be formed to fit the broken limb and held in place with Ace bandages, Vet wrap, or rags. It is the preferred splinting device for wilderness travel and occupies very little room in an aid bag.

Vetwrap. Also known as Co-Flex and Co-Ban, it is similar to an Ace bandage but is much easier to use because it sticks to itself. It can also be cut up to form small bandages.

Oral rehydration salts. These are the best treatment for dehydration and diarrhea in the wilderness. Simply mix with a liter of water and have the patient drink slowly. During a filming venture in South America, oral rehydration salts saved me from severe dehydration after a two-day bout with food poisoning. Just like the EpiPen, this is one item that no travel first-aid kit should be without.

Oral glucose gel and tablets. These are great for travelers with diabetes who might suffer from an insulin reaction as well as travelers suffering from sugar deficiencies brought on by dehydration. These can be safely used anytime such chemical imbalances are suspected in the patient.

Other items in our kit include latex gloves, various syringe and needle sizes, EMT shears, hemostats, cold wrap, suture kits, oral thermometer, Sawyers Extractor, and a comprehensive wound-care package. Medications include prescription pain killers (both codeine and noncodeine based), prescription antibiotics (including Cipro), prescription metronidazole for intestinal parasites such as Giardia, prescription lariam, prescription lidocaine local anesthetic, prescription lamisil anti-fungal cream, Purell gelled alcohol, and Benadryl. We usually buy our trip antibiotics and meds in-country, then ditch what we don't use before we leave.

One final tip: a lot of first-aid supplies can be purchased through veterinary supply houses for much cheaper than what you would pay for them through standard medical suppliers. For example, we buy our Vetwrap—which is the exact same thing as hospital Co-Flex—for *a lot* less money by going through veterinary supply stores. You can also purchase epinephrine (treatment for bee sting reactions and anaphylactic shock) directly from these outlets, where you would need a prescription to buy it from your local pharmacy. This is the same epinephrine (1:1000) as found in an EpiPen, although it is labeled "not for human use." Needles, syringes, skin staplers, suture kits, and other tools can also be purchased through vet suppliers at a discount rate.

DISEASE-FREE TRAVEL

Before you begin your travels, always check with the Centers for Disease Control to get the latest updates on your destination areas. (The CDC is on the Web at http://www.cdc.gov/, or write them at 1600 Clifton Road, Atlanta, GA, 30333.) Some countries may require certain vaccinations before entrance is granted. Proof of vaccination is obtained through the medical facility performing the vaccinations in the form of an International Certificate of Vaccination as approved by the World Heath Organization. This yellow card should stay with your passport at all times because it contains medical information about you.

Your local doctor or health-care facility will usually be the final say on what diseases you need to protect against before you travel, but in any tropical Third World country it's always safe to have vaccinations for hepatitis (various strains), typhoid, and yellow fever and boosters for MMR (mumps, measles, rubella) and tetanus. You may also need prescriptions to guard against malaria, which usually comes in the form of a once-a-week oral tablet called lariam or a once-a-day capsule of doxycycline.

As discussed earlier, if you should get sick and need to visit a hospital for an injection, request that they use your personal needles and syringes from your first-aid kit. Third World mentality is to make use of everything as much as possible before throwing it away, so you may end up being treated with a dirty needle otherwise. This is a deadly gamble, especially in developing countries where diseases such as AIDS and hepatitis are running rampant. We once witnessed doctors using the same syringe to medicate two different patients. The syringe was aspirated on the first patient during injection, which caused a backflow of blood into the syringe. Then a new needle was placed on the same syringe and used on the next patient.

Possibly the biggest threat to travelers is waterborne diseases. Throughout our numerous trips into the Third World, we have had team members contract a myriad of waterborne problems. Giardia seems to be the most recurring and can be very difficult to diagnose. As a precaution, always purify any water you drink overseas. This can be done with iodine-based purifiers (liquid or tablet form), chlorine, or pump-type water filters. Also remember that brushing your teeth with tap water or having ice in your drinks can be just as bad as drinking the water directly.

Another common problem is food-based sicknesses. Although most of these are mild reactions due to change in diet, sometimes they can develop into severe cases of diarrhea or food poisoning. Many foods are undercooked in developing countries and can carry parasites and other nasty bugs that may make you sick. Refrigeration is typically nonexistent in remote villages, and meat preservation is usually done by a process of salting and smoking. We have eaten many pieces of meat that were covered with flies and larvae just before being cooked. The rule of thumb is to always be sure wild foods are thoroughly cooked and fruit is always peeled before sticking it in your mouth.

If you do develop a case of food poisoning, do your best to stay hydrated. Drinking clear liquids, taking oral rehydration salts, and slowly reverting back to a solid diet will usually get you through the ordeal. As insurance we always carry prescription ciprofloxacin hydrochloride, which seems to knock out just about any nasty bug that comes along.

Wound infections can be very serious while overseas. Back home, most of us hardly pay any attention to minor cuts and scrapes; if we do anything at all, we usually just apply a Band-Aid to stop any annoying bleeding. Once you're overseas, this practice has to change. Your body's immune system basically undergoes a certain amount of trauma once it's introduced into a new world with its new bugs, new climate, and new diet, so even minor wounds must be given immediate care as soon as they occur. Even tiny bug and mosquito bites can develop into raging infections if scratched continually. A good triple antibiotic ointment coupled with proper wound cleansing and dressing is the best insurance policy a traveler can have.

When traveling, also remember that disease goes in both directions. We have been to areas that few white men have ever seen, yet we've always kept in mind the fact that the indigenous population could easily be susceptible to things that do not fatally affect us. A common cold or a flu bug taken into such places has the potential to wipe out many people. An acquaintance of ours once bragged about visiting a very remote tribe of people while suffering from the flu. The proper thing would have been to wait until the bug had passed before going in. We never found out if this affected the tribe, but it does demonstrate the contempt that some people from the "civilized" world have for indigenous people trying to survive under already

Remember that disease travels both ways once you interject yourself into Third World. The Urarina people shown in this photo have had very little contact with the civilized world. Bringing something such as the flu into this tribe could be devastating.

difficult conditions. Idiots like this need to find other adventures to brag about.

Keep this in mind and notify your guide or traveling partners of any condition you have that may affect the area you're going into. If you are ill, keep your visits as short as possible, and do your best to avoid contact altogether with those who may be susceptible to Western bugs and illnesses. If in doubt, minimize as much personal contact as you can. It's just not worth the photo or video you might get.

FIRST-AID TRAINING

Of course, emergency first aid can be much more complex than the procedures described in this chapter. Evacuation and rescue techniques can be just as crucial, if not more, than the first aid given on the scene. If your trip includes very remote backcountry travel, we highly suggest acquiring Wilderness First Aid (WFA) certification at a minimum. A WFA course covers all the basics, from initial assessment to delivering the victim into the hands of qualified medical personnel. Throughout the course an instructor answers students' questions, drills them on critical areas and techniques, and teaches them how and what to pack in their aid bags. Students are also provided a comprehensive Wilderness First Aid manual by the National Safety Council and the Wilderness Medical Society. This manual is an easy read and takes the caregiver step-by-step through proper assessment and treatment of a casualty.

Although the majority of this first-aid section comes from direct field time and a WFA course, we also consulted an acquaintance of ours, Myke Hawkeye, for his expert opinion on the subject. Myke is a Special Forces medic and Chief of Field Operations for Global Univision's Special Operations Medical Services. He has acquired much experience and field time in many less-than-desirable places around the world. His words illustrate the focus of this chapter rather well:

"Having been in the bush with many different types of people, I have consistently noted that those who do not factor any accidents, injuries, or illnesses into their mission planning most often sustain some such malady, while those who do consider the everpresent possibility of them, and make ready accordingly, almost never incur them and rarely are required to implement their course of action. Hence, to not plan for failure is to plan for failure."

Myke adds, "In the course of pursuing any study, one should attempt to seek the highest level of authority for the subject matter at hand. Then they should get all the knowledge and training as is available to them. Then, if feasible, review that which is one or two levels above their means. In this way, they will have an idea of how best to proceed with their own implementation by knowing how the next courses of action will follow. Hence, know the basics, study the advanced, understand the rest."

C H A P T E R   1 1

The Trip Home

For us, the hardest part of any adventure trip is leaving the host country and returning to the rat race of "civilized" living. After spending time with indigenous people, you develop a form of kinship with them that's difficult to walk away from. You even begin to feel a bond with the shysters and con artists, especially when you realize that the motivation behind their antics is nothing more than a form of survival. Even during times of war and civil unrest, there's something about this frontier life that every adventurer feels at peace with and seems to have a desire to be part of.

Be that as it may, reality dictates that you don't belong there, and most of us have to be content with just visiting every once in a while, receiving our adrenaline fix, then getting back to the 9-to-5 grind at home.

Just because the trip is over and you feel like you've been through hell and survived it, it doesn't mean you should lose your sense of awareness. On our trips, the last night almost always ends up as a party night for the new guys, resulting in hangovers, headaches, and having to drag them away from their newfound female friends. Instead of taking the final night to carefully repack their gear, many of them wait until the last minute to throw everything in their packs. Upon arriving at the airport, they can't find their passports, immigration papers, or anything else they had protected with their lives throughout the trip. Some forget to remove knives from their pockets, which causes a stir at security on the way to the gate, while others swagger in still half drunk, with a cocky attitude toward everything. There's always one in every group, and being trip leaders we never fully relax until we have the whole crew corralled on the flight back to the United States.

If it's not enough dealing with final-day chaos, just wait until your perfectly planned schedule gets screwed. When it comes to dealing with airlines, especially local carriers, you're at their mercy, and there's no guarantee of getting home on time. On several occasions we have had flights canceled out from under us, which caused us to miss connections and created a rescheduling nightmare. We've also sat on the tarmac for hours at a time waiting for fog to lift from our connecting airport; been evacuated and quarantined because of a bomb on board; flown several hundred miles out of the way to deliver parts to a stranded airliner in a jungle town; and had to subdue an irate passenger over the middle of the Pacific Ocean, thus rerouting our plane for a nonscheduled stop in Japan.

The only advice we can offer is to always reconfirm your flights at least 24 hours in advance. It doesn't matter if you have a guaranteed ticket; many Third World airlines will book your seat to someone else if you don't reconfirm within a certain amount of time. Even worse, some will cancel flights at the last minute if they don't have enough passengers, causing you to miss your connecting flight home. If this happens, always call the carrier of your connecting flight and let them know you will not be able to get on your scheduled flight. Many airlines have a rule that requires you to cancel a confirmed reservation if you will not be using it for any reason. If you don't, you run the risk of forfeiting your ticket.

Having said that, we have flown all the major international carriers and missed flights with confirmed reservations and have never had to purchase a new ticket to get ourselves home. As mentioned earlier in this book, always try to purchase all of your tickets from a reputable travel agent, or at least use a major credit card. If the carrier goes bankrupt, at least you will have a means of getting your money back. (Don't think this is a far-fetched idea—it's happened to us twice during our travels. On one of our trips we actually had an aircraft repossessed at the gate. It seems the carrier was way behind in paying creditors so they took the plane, leaving the passengers to figure out their own way home.)

If there's one thing we have stressed throughout this book, it's to be self-sufficient when traveling. So if you're a souvenir shopper, never buy more than you can haul or take care of yourself. Once you arrive at the airport, mind your own luggage at all times. If you are traveling with a group, let them know where you are going if you wander off. Many times we've had people walk around the airport or take taxis downtown without anyone else. The worst part about this is that they usually leave their luggage sitting in a corner, expecting everyone else to take care of their stuff, then get upset when something comes up missing. Receiving help from your traveling companions is fine as long as they are willing and it doesn't hinder the rest of the scheduled trip.

After arriving at the airport, we usually throw all the luggage in one pile and take turns watching it so everyone can go eat, smoke, souvenir shop, or use the bathroom. If your wait is going to be very long, find a secure storage area with lockers to pack your gear in. There's nothing worse than toting packs all over an airport waiting for the ticket desk to open and take the stuff off your hands. If you do wander away from your luggage, always keep your passport, tickets, and papers on your person just in case you're stopped and asked to identify yourself by airport security.

In many foreign countries, you will have to pay an airport tax to leave the country. This is usually taken care of at another area of the airport and not at the ticket desk. I don't know how many times I've been in line to go through security and had to wait because some idiot didn't follow the rules and forgot to pay the departure tax. You are not going to get out of the country without paying the taxes, so always have the right amount of money set aside and be sure you don't spend it inadvertently.

Finally, once you go through security and arrive at your gate, put your boarding pass in a location where you will be able to find it. Yes, as silly as this sounds, we've had folks lose their boarding passes while standing in line to get on the plane.

I realize that a lot of these tips seem to be common sense, but you would be surprised at the idiotic things we have seen pulled at airports. It seems like adventure travelers always lose their heads right before returning home. Maybe it's from the anticipation of seeing their families, the invincible feeling of enduring a trip most folks couldn't, or maybe they were just nutty all along, but being trip leaders we feel a responsibility to be guardian angel over folks who can't take care of themselves. If you don't think you can hold it together on this final stage of your journey, be sure to travel with a good guide or trusted companion who will watch over you.

REPATRIATION INTO YOUR COUNTRY OF ORIGIN

Going back into the United States is about the same as entering any country. If you're a U.S. citizen, you will only be required to fill out a Customs declaration detailing the goods you are bringing back. If all you're hauling is souvenirs, make a close estimate of their value and tally it up on the back of the form. Once you get off the plane, follow the line to Immigrations, then on to Customs to reclaim your baggage and pass through the inspectors. Do not use your cell phone or photographic equipment in these areas. I don't know why but U.S. officials get upset about this, so save the phone call home until you get through Customs.

For the most part, you will not experience the smiling faces of officials like you did when you entered the foreign country. In fact, I'm beginning to believe that part of the training for any federal "security" position is how to appear menacing and disrespectful. For some reason, employees at U.S. ports and borders take their jobs way too seriously and think that everyone should be treated like suspected criminals, especially if they're coming out of a country known for drug trafficking or terrorist activity. Pay no mind to their surly attitude, and let it pass when they don't say "please," "thank you," or "I'm sorry" when they screw up. Answer any questions you are asked, let them inspect what they want to, and then go about your business. Just be glad you don't have their jobs because most of the badges you see on the floor are simple inspectors and not Customs agents. Dealing with them is similar to dealing with rent-a-cop security guards as compared to dealing with real law-enforcement officers—a complete contrast in professionalism.

If you're hauling in a load of souvenirs that have the potential to be considered contraband, expect close inspection of your goods. Many insect and animal products, for example, are on the banned list even in souvenir form. If you have something to hide, you will probably be noticed, definitely inspected, and possibly pulled for a secondary search. To avoid these delays, carefully select any items you bring home, and leave anything that's doubtful or could raise suspicion. You would be surprised what people try to smuggle in—everything from live marmosets and snakes to full-sized jaguar hides hidden in their hair or pants or wrapped in their luggage.

Also be careful of pharmaceuticals that may be legally acquired over the counter in foreign countries but illegal without a prescription in the United States. We usually buy our trip antibiotics and meds once we're in-country, then ditch what we don't use before we leave.

Whatever you do, never haul anything back through Customs for one of your traveling companions unless you are absolutely sure about its legality, and never, ever try to bribe any U.S. official. Unlike some Third World countries, these guys make a decent living and will nail your ass for smuggling, attempted bribery, or any other charge you're stupid enough to bring on yourself. The absolute rules when dealing with U.S. Customs are to be legal, be courteous, and follow their directions. Do this and you will never have reentry problems and possibly never make it on their watch list.

A good friend of ours who is a U.S. Customs agent gave this advice for the readers of this book: "For purposes of avoiding problems, I'd advise readers to always stash copies of their passport and tickets as well as any prescriptions for medicine, etc., in their luggage in case of loss of original documents. It'll save a lot of aggravation later on. Advise them to declare goods honestly and be polite, but not be too eager to engage inspectors in conversation. Having proper documents ready to go, plus a backup set, is the best insurance against trouble. Basically, those who don't violate laws have nothing to fear. Of course there is always the possibility of a secondary examination, but that's just procedure."

In conclusion, you are responsible for determining what is legal and what is not when dealing with any material coming in from overseas. Maintain control of your own bags, know exactly what is in them at all times, and never leave them for one moment in the company of strangers or even with any traveling companion you don't know very well. If something does go wrong on your return—such as a kilo of cocaine mysteriously ending up in your bag—remain calm and secure a lawyer before answering *any* questions.

POST-TRIP HEALTH CONCERNS

Getting physically sick when traveling is not just limited to your time in foreign countries. In fact, if your trip is only a couple of weeks long, you're more likely to get sick after you return home. The reasons for this vary, but mainly it's due to the gestation periods of some bugs and the extreme change in diet once you return to the States. Americans are known for eating fatty, heavily seasoned foods. Going from this type of diet to a more bland menu usually doesn't have too many ill effects, but going the opposite way does cause some problems. Once your system acclimates to a bland diet, it taxes it to suddenly throw a Burger King Whopper in the mix. We suggest slowly returning to your normal diet by gradually reducing your intake of bland foods such as rice and beans while slowly increasing your consumption of your usual foods.

The second post-trip medical concern is disease and par-

Third World travel is exhilarating, addictive, and an awakening experience to how the rest of the world lives. Grasping the reality of the Third World can only be done through personal travel there because it bears no resemblance to what the major media portray.

asite flare-ups. As mentioned previously, bugs such as Giardia and other internal parasites may go undetected for some time and are hard to diagnose if the doctor is not looking for them. If a botfly bites you and lays eggs in your skin during the last few days of the trip, expect a lump and live maggots underneath by the time you get home. Diseases such as malaria and blood flukes are no different. All of

Acknowledgments and Resources

This book has been a long time coming, and we're happy to finally see it through and be able to offer it to fellow adventurers. As these last pages are being written, we're finalizing plans for another expedition into one of the world's most dangerous places—the jungles of southern Colombia. Hopefully, planning, organizing, and following our own advice will allow us to return safely and with a better understanding of the conflict there and the people who make up this beautiful area of the world.

Before we head out, we want to mention a few folks who deserve recognition, not only for their help with this book but also for their support during our travels. Special thanks to you guys for your trust, friendship, and advice. It's been a wild ride so far, and I hope we all spur a lot more out of the chutes before sucking our last breath. See you on the trail!

Robert Young Pelton. As the author of the best-selling books *The World's Most Dangerous Places*, *Come Back Alive*, *The Adventurist*, and *The Hunter, The Hammer, and Heaven*, Robert has traveled the world over in search of adventure and truth in less-than-desirable locations. He has traveled with the Taliban in Afghanistan before the recent U.S. war against that group (and was the first person to interview American Taliban fighter John Walker after he was detained in Afghanistan), survived a plane crash in Borneo, narrowly escaped a terrorist bombing in Africa, and ducked incoming artillery while reporting from the front lines of the Chechnya/Russia conflict. Robert also hosts "The World's Most Dangerous Places" television series for the Travel Channel. He is considered a leading expert on travel in dangerous locations and has been interviewed on numerous occasions by the major networks. His advice, writings, and beer-drinking sessions with us in dark corners of the world have been instrumental to the content of this book. We consider his travel guides the best money can buy for hard-core adventurers. For more information, visit his Web site at www.comebackalive.com.

Ted Nugent and the Randall's Adventure & Training team. Left to right: Patricia Tadder, Mike Perrin, Jeff Randall, Ted Nugent.

Ted Nugent. Our thanks to rock-and-roll superstar, avid outdoorsman, and friend Ted Nugent for reviewing this book. Through his organization, United Sportsmen of America, Ted has been *the* voice for hunters, shooters, and outdoorsmen for years. He has traveled the world performing on stage and hunting in the bush, keeping the spirit of America and the wilderness alive and well. Ted has also worked side-by-side with politicians to protect the rights of outdoorsmen and adventurers the world over. If you are serious about the outdoors, then get involved with his organization. It's an investment that will pay for itself for generations to come. For more information on Ted Nugent United Sportsmen of America, visit their Web site at www.tednugent.com or write to them at 4008 West Michigan Avenue, Jackson, MI, 49202.

Bill Johnson. A long-time friend of the authors, Bill Johnson dropped out of medical school determined to volunteer as a medic with the Afghan rebels fighting Soviet invasion forces in Afghanistan in the 1980s. He continued his patriotic travels working as a medic for the Nicaraguan freedom fighters (the Contras), then labored in a South African factory alongside the Zulu and Xhosa to learn firsthand about the effects of apartheid in that country. After traveling the world, he finally returned to Alabama and settled into politics, becoming a city councilman in Birmingham and heading up various political campaigns. His input and advice have been a tremendous help throughout our travels and the writing of this book. For more information on Bill, go to www.billjohnson.org.

Cresson Kearney. Thanks to Cresson for the phone conversations, insight, and years of experience working in adverse conditions while training men to do the impossible and be successful at their missions. His book, *Jungle Snafus and Remedies*, has been instrumental in our quest to design and implement better gear for hostile environments. If your travels will take you into the jungle or tropical areas, his book is a must read.

Darryl Patton. A member of our South American team, Darryl Patton is the publisher of *Stalking The Wild*, a magazine devoted to the outdoors and the primitive skills of our ancestors. Darryl has led classes in primitive and wilderness survival for many years in both the United States and South America. Although his passion and main area of expertise is in edible and medicinal plants, he teaches classes on all aspects of primitive skills. For many years, Darryl was privileged to study under Tommie Bass, one of the last of the old mountain herb doctors. During this time, he learned about the special properties of literally thousands of plants from Mr. Bass along with how to make old-time teas, tonics, and salves from what nature offered. Darryl is the author of *Tommie Bass: Herb Doctor of Shinbone Ridge*, *America's Goat Man*, and *Grandpa Whiting's Mountain Medi-*

cine. Whether you want to learn how to brain-tan a deer hide, make fire with a hand drill, or simply live off the land armed only with a knife and your wits, Darryl has classes designed to teach you these skills. For more information, visit his Web site at www.stalkingthewild.com or write him at Stalking The Wild, P.O. Box 8481, Gadsden, AL, 35902.

Jerry VanCook. Being an author for Paladin Press, Jerry was the original inspiration for us to sit down and write this book. He has worked side-by-side with us in the South American jungles, both instructed and received training from various militaries of that region, and has authored numerous articles and books on the subject of personal defense, including *Going Undercover*. This classic how-to book for undercover cops is more than just that— it's a blueprint for anyone who wishes to learn the art of role camouflage. Chapter after chapter teaches the simple yet subtle psychology necessary to project the image you desire and create illusions of reality. Like Miyomoto Musashi's *Go Rin No Sho* (better known as *A Book of Five Rings*), Jerry's book is adaptable not only to police work but business practices, security and self-defense, and many other areas of life. Another excellent piece of work is his book *Real World Self-Defense*; Jerry's many years on the street as an undercover cop gave him the real-world fighting experience to write it. Combining a long and impressive background in both the Eastern and Western fighting arts, he strips away the myths and frills of fancy self-defense and gets down to the simple core that works. For beginner and expert alike, if you can own only one self-defense book for today's society, this is the one.

The government, people, and air force of Peru. Although we have traveled to just about every corner of the world, the country of Peru has become our second home. Through many years of working side by side with its military and indigenous people, we have been able to hone our wilderness and adventure travel skills in its incredible jungle, part of the largest and most diverse jungle on Earth.

Peruvian military officials and Randall's
Adventure & Training's jungle survival instructors.

Peru is an adventurer's paradise, offering the diversity of
rain forests, desert, and high mountainous regions. One
word of warning, though: Once you go the first time, you'll
be making the trip back for the rest of your life. Special
thanks to the Escuela de Supervivencia en La Selva (school
of jungle survival), Commandante Mendoza, and the officers and enlisted men of Group 42 Air Force.

**The government and people of Costa Rica and the
Osa Peninsula.** Although our operations span nearly every
country in Central and South America, Costa Rica has
become another second home for us. If you're looking for a

place to get away from all the tourists and still maintain most of the luxuries of home, check out the lesser known paradise of Carate, a village on the Osa Peninsula. This area offers hiking, gold panning, kayaking, and horseback riding in the middle of the most awesome triple-canopy jungle, turquoise surf, and black sand beaches you will ever see. Whether you go by automobile or plane, you will travel through a small town called Puerto Jimenez. Once you get there, look up our amigo Adolfo Preuss and tell him we sent you. He'll be easy to find since everyone in town knows him. Adolfo speaks perfect English and Spanish and has a nice little establishment named Terrapin Lodge. Adolfo is an expert when it comes to jungle and survival travel. This is one trip that won't cost you a lot of money and you will talk about for years to come.

Randall's Adventure & Training. The authors are partners in Randall's Adventure & Training (RAT), an adventure/training business with operations and personnel in Central and South America. RAT offers tropical survival and downed pilot training as well as remote jungle expeditions for civilians, law-enforcement and military personnel, and film crews from all over the world. RAT is also considered a leading company in the research and design of military and civilian gear for jungle and extremely adverse environments. For more information, visit RAT on the Web at www.jungle-training.com or contact them at 60 Randall Road, Gallant, AL 35972. For a virtual campfire discussion format hosted by RAT, visit www.jungletraining.com/ forums.

SPECOPS. The folks at SPECOPS have been friends of the authors for a long time. They have instructed for our company, and we have instructed for theirs. SPECOPS is an adventure, outdoor skills, and survival education group composed of U.S. Army Special Forces veterans. Their cadre of seasoned guides and instructors combine years of real-world experience with a multitude of skills to provide the most unique and professionally organized adventures and training programs available. Utilizing a global network of

Special Operations veterans, they offer multilingual programs in executive protection security services; adventure, extreme, and educational tourism; medical, language, and security support for the film industry; and outdoor skills and survival courses across the United States. For more information, go to www.specops.com or write them at 6604 Midnight Pass Road, Sarasota, FL, 34242.

Brigade Quartermasters. Any adventure outing is only as good as the equipment you take. Mitch Werbell IV and his company, Brigade Quartermasters, have been a part of our team since the beginning. Their business philosophy has always been to supply quality gear at reasonable prices on time. The staff at BQ are not your typical wannabe warrior surplus salesmen—they use what they sell and have years of military, adventure, and travel experience under their belts. We would like to express our thanks to them for going above and beyond in their support of our operations, and also for outfitting us during our sometimes unorthodox methods of adventure travel. For more information, go to www.actiongear.com or write Brigade Quartermasters, P.O. Box 100001, 1025 Cobb International Drive NW, Ste. 100, Kennesaw, GA, 30156-9217.

Jim Six. The authors wish to express their thanks to Jim Six for the initial edit of this book and making our gibberish more reader friendly. Jim is a feature columnist and senior writer for the *Gloucester County Times* in Woodbury, New Jersey. Jim started his writing career in 1964 at the *Philadelphia Evening Bulletin*. In his varied career, he has been a print and broadcast newsman and has won numerous journalism awards, including honors for his feature column, music reviews, news features, and deadline reporting on hard news stories. He has slugged 25-year-old Scotch with Willie Nelson, ridden an 1,800-pound bull at the rodeo, had drinks with Buffalo Bill's grandson, received death threats from drug lords, and covered various special operations units during his action-packed career. For more information on Jim and his writings, go to www.jim.six.org.

Special thanks to our many adventurous clients who are still wondering why they paid us good money to endure such misery. We would also like to thank the following for their input and help in various ways: Mike Fuller, John Greco, Newt Livesay, Ontario Knife Co., Luis Icomena, Michael Benish, Myke Hawkeye, Larry Myers, Jon Ford, Steven Dick, Paladin Press, and Harris Publications. Also thanks to the various U.S. military units who have beat the hell out of our gear and helped us to design a better product with their input. *Muchas gracias, amigos!*

Of course, there are other folks who cannot be mentioned by name due to their current employment with government agencies or operational status overseas. However, there is one retired agent from Alabama who is due a huge amount of thanks for "encouraging" us to pursue the right path. Thanks, Bill R. The rest know who they are, and we thank you for saving our ass and squeaking us through the cracks on more than one occasion. As always, the beer is on us when we meet again.

Last but not least, we want to thank our families for encouraging and enduring our unique and sometimes strange lifestyle. Without support from home, none of our travels would be worth the effort.

Salud! Travel safe, and enjoy life!

About the Authors

Robert Young Pelton (left) and author Jeff Randall in South America during the filming of a segment of Pelton's "World's Most Dangerous Places" television series.

Randall's Adventure & Training team members Patricia Tadder (left)
and author Mike Perrin about to go over the edge during a
RAT high-angle ropes training class.

Jeff Randall has made dozens of international trips to
nearly every country in Central and South America. He has
also worked and traveled in China, Korea, Malaysia,
Indonesia, Singapore, Switzerland, and many other countries in between. Jeff has organized and participated in
filming ventures with major media outlets, worked with
Special Operations military personnel during training sessions, instructed wilderness survival courses to students of
all ages, and arranged and participated in training classes
with foreign militaries and police organizations. A former
law-enforcement officer, Jeff is a graduate of the Peruvian
Air Force's Jungle Operations and Survival School, an NRA
certified pistol and personal defense instructor, and an

instructor in high-angle SRT (single-rope techniques) and basic mountaineering skills. He is certified in Wilderness First Aid by the National Safety Council and has assisted in wilderness first-aid training classes for indigenous people and officials in South America. An accomplished amateur photographer, he is a contributing editor for *Tactical Knives* magazine and the author of its survival column. He is also frequently published in *American Survival Guide*, *Costa Rica Outdoors*, *Modern Survival*, and numerous other publications. He and coauthor Mike Perrin have been quoted experts on the subject of jungle survival for numerous publications, books, and films. Jeff is well recognized within the military and hard-core adventure crowd due to his constant research and development of better gear. He speaks intermediate Spanish and is a continuing student of the language.

Mike Perrin is an avid outdoorsman and has made numerous trips into the cities and jungles of Central and South America. He is a graduate of the Peruvian Air Force's Jungle Operations and Survival School and a wilderness survival instructor specializing in tropical environments. He is an NRA certified pistol and personal defense instructor and is experienced in high-angle rope techniques. He speaks basic Spanish and continues to study the language. He is certified in luck, having escaped many situations that should have killed him. In his spare time, Mike researches and designs gear for extreme environments. Many of his projects and designs are well-recognized within the hard-core adventure community, most notably knives built by custom and production makers for Randall's Adventure & Training.